REAL
CIDERMAKING
ON A SMALL SCALE

REAL CIDERMAKING
ON A SMALL SCALE

Michael Pooley & John Lomax

An Amateur Winemaker Book

Special Interest Model Books Ltd.
P.O. Box 327
Poole
Dorset
BH15 2RG
England

First published by Nexus Special Interest Ltd. 1999

This edition published by Special Interest Model Books Ltd. 2002

Reprinted 2004, 2005, 2007 (twice), 2008, 2009, 2010

ISBN 978-1-85486-195-5

www.specialinterestmodelbooks.co.uk

Printed and bound in Malta by Melita Press

Contents

Acknowledgements

Moonlit Apples is reproduced by permission of the estate of John Drinkwater and Samuel French Ltd.

Thanks and acknowledgements are extended to Maggie Mason for use of illustrations on pages 5, 77, 100 and 101 , to Miri Hastilow for permission to use photographs on pages 3, 6, 23, 38, 39, 45, 52, 61, 76 and 82, and to Dave, Sue and Steve Halford for permission to use the photographs on pages 14, 25, 34, 98 and 106.

Thanks are also extended to Geoff Warren of The Three Counties Cider & Perry Association for helpful comments on the text and to *The Shropshire Star* for permission to use the illustration on the back cover.

Moonlit Apples

At the top of the house the apples are laid in rows,
And the skylight lets the moonlight in, and those
Apples are deep-sea apples of green. There goes
    A cloud on the moon in the autumn night.

A mouse in the wainscot scratches, and scratches, and then
There is no sound at the top of the house of men
Or mice, and the cloud is blown, and the moon again
    Dapples the apples with deep-sea light.

They are lying in rows there, under the gloomy beams;
On the sagging floor, they gather the silver streams
Out of the moon, those moonlit apples of dreams,
    And quiet is the steep stair under.

In the corridors under there is nothing but sleep.
And stiller than ever on orchard boughs they keep
Tryst with the moon, and deep in the silence, deep
    On moon-washed apples of wonder.

John Drinkwater   1882–1937

1 Introduction

'Oh, not cidermaking again already?' we protest . . . 'All that cutting up and pounding of apples! We've still got the bruises on our hands from last year!'

(But secretly we like it!)

A number of reasons have inspired this practical guide to small-scale cidermaking. The hope is that it will provide anyone who is at least faintly interested in the craft with the skills and incentive to turn apples – especially those that might otherwise go to waste – into a quite deli-cious drink, while at the same time helping to stimulate the further cultivation and use of the fruit.

One thing leads to another. As more and more people begin to make cider, so thoughts of shaping the idea into a wider community enterprise with small community orchards and perhaps even a community press will grow. The apple is at home in any temperate climate, particularly the British climate, but compared to 30 or 40 years ago, so many varieties having become exhausted or lost through wholesale grubbing up of orchards, the need to promote apple culture is more pressing than ever. The organisation, Common Ground, has probably done most in recent years to remind people of the enormous richness of their apple cultures, and the threats posed by large-scale agribusiness and modern retailing patterns, so that there is now a resurgence of interest in the fruit. 'Apple Day' in Britain (21 October) was started by Common Ground a few years ago and has now entered the calendar as a fixed date in celebration of this culture. It is hugely popular, so much so that the idea is already being adopted in many other countries around the world.

Such trends testify to the fruit's importance, of which cider is just one vital strand. Until recently, this had been particularly neglected, both the cause and effect of which was, to a large extent, a poor commercial product. Now there is a revival in the real product, and the hope is that this book can make its contribution to the process.

In the following pages you will find plans and information needed to build a sturdy press, the skills and confidence to make real cider, and a sustaining idea that to do so at this level, is, in its modest way, to continue an ancient rural craft. Not least of the book's messages is that in the doing and the making, there is an enormous amount of fun to be had. Small-scale cidermaking can be a wonderful communal activity – low-tech and in need of people. We should celebrate the fact that it is labour intensive, as there is a case for doing so with much other work in society, instead of the seemingly inevitable displacement of people in favour of machines. The physical labour in cidermaking itself is satisfying because it is earthy, shared, varied and directed to some splendid product, while the occasion – whether you live in an urban or rural environment – is full of rich social and recreational possibilities for adults and children alike engaged upon a common enterprise.

Whether you have fruit from just one or two trees in the garden, or a positive embarrassment of apples each autumn from a small orchard, or even access to much larger supplies, the hope is that the book will inspire you to make cider. Of course, voracious children, apple pies, storage, freezing, or those donations to 'less fortunate' neighbours and relatives can, assuming you have the time, all make inroads into the surplus. For most people, however, often for want of seeing how or being able to deal with the apples, the majority of the fruit will simply rot, or be left for the birds and slugs to gorge themselves on. It is true, that in that sense they are not being wasted, for slugs, too, have their role to play in the great cycle of life, but in other important senses it is a waste and most people want better for their apples.

This book will show you how to see them right. Good cidermaking!

Operating two small-scale presses at a communal cidermaking day.

2 A Word on Apples

The wild crab is solitary, found in woods or roadside hedges. Its blossom is lovely as any, but the smell of its fallen fruit on a winter's day walk, when thoughts of apples have long been left behind, is so delicious it might tempt you as legend has it. Would you bite into a crab apple? It would bite you back with interest!

The apple is an astonishing creation. Sow a pip and each time it would grow to bear a different variety. The ancestry of the cultivated fruit as we know it today, *Malus pumila domestica*, leads back through the ages to the wild crab from the Caucasus region of modern Georgia. Thousands of years of hybridisation and grafting experiments by human beings, along with processes of natural selection, have resulted in a fruit of such rich genetic make-up that the number of possible varieties is quite staggering.

Everything flows from this complex history. The apple is quite exceptional among fruits in having such diversity of

The International Apple Tree, New Zealand bears 118 varieties from 31 countries

shape and colour, texture and flavour, or cropping season, considering all the varieties involved. There are more cultivars of the apple than any other fruit of similar importance, and although most are at home in a cool temperate climate, few places in the world – barring the tropics themselves – are unwelcoming of at least one variety or another.

In Britain today hundreds of different examples still thrive (though sometimes one might be forgiven for doubting this), and over the centuries as many as 6,000 or more have been bred or chanced upon. The likelihood, however, of our sown pip ever yielding a variety of any worth is extremely small, for those that we have come to value for this reason or that, adapted to this locality or that, have been arrived at by the amateur grower's or the professional plant breeder's arts of ruthless selection and rejection. Those that we do value are sweet to eat, cook well, make excellent cider, resist disease and frosts, crop heavily, are aesthetic of shape and colour and so on. The vast majority of the many varieties still to be found in Britain are local in the sense of being distinctive to an area, or even unique to a parish or neighbourhood according to the nature of the soil, climate, and the particularities of circumstance that brought them into being at all.

A tubful of mixed apples ready for washing prior to cutting up, milling and pressing.

The long tradition of selecting for new qualities in the apple continues apace today. There are many examples of successful modern cultivars, but despite our century's frequent contempt for the past, the truth is that the best varieties are still the old ones. And behind each one, perhaps intimated in the name, lies the story: the chance discovery, the painstaking work, the labour of love of the individual from which could arise such splendid dessert apples as an Ashmead's Kernel or a Cox's Orange Pippin, or that most famous of culinary apples, the Bramley's Seedling, raised in a Nottinghamshire cottage garden by Betsy Brailsford sometime between 1809 and 1813. Where the seed came from isn't known, but the original tree is still there, thriving.

Just as rich as the apple itself is the body of literature, music, art, folk stories, recipes, sayings and myths that have come to surround the fruit. Its very ordinariness is its richness, the fact that it is such a commonplace thing the reason why it touches people, enters so extensively the language and culture and has come to be used to symbolise so many different aspects of our lives.

The apple picked too young is tart; left to mature, becomes the very epitome of ripeness; often embodies a kind of homeliness 'as a Kerry pippin to crack and crunch', a comeliness as the tree that 'leans down low at Linden Lee', as ruddy a panacea of good health (at least in keeping the doctor away). If some people wrinkle with age as an 'apple-john', are crabbed of personality, or enjoy a way life that is often sweet one side, bitter on the other, there are also those cherished as the Psalmist's 'apple of an eye'. Some things are just in 'apple-pie order', as important not to be upset as the carefully laid 'cart'; some offers as tempting (and perhaps as dire if taken up) as Eve's; some insights as ordinary and profound as Newton's supposed route to gravity; some historical figures as memorable as William Tell, some events as portentous as his exploits. The symbols and stories are seemingly endless.

The etymology of the word apple is also as fascinating as unresolved. The major European languages, apart from the Romance languages, have words for the fruit which are prefixed *ap-*, *ab-*, or similar alternatives, but all curiously seem to predate or find no origin in any Indo-European root. (The Arabic *al-* seems suggestive but it is

Apple blossom on a large Bramley's Seedling tree.

difficult to establish any credible route.) That other Indo-European-rooted language, Latin, has an alternative etymology, giving us *malus*, derived from the Greek *mailon*. Perhaps just as the word cider itself formerly denoted fermented drinks from a whole range of fruits, or even Eve's offer from the garden of a fruit rather than an apple, so *mailon* appears not so much a cognate in Greek of apple as the generic for fruit, though the word is still retained in English, specifically in melon.

3 Cidermaking History

Little wonder there are so many alcoholic drinks. Sugars and starches in fruits and cereals are disposed to ferment naturally and the formation of cider is no exception. It is possible that cider has existed in some form for almost as long as there have been apples – say, a few thousand years.

Perhaps something of the real antiquity of the drink is held in the widespread tradition of its communal drinking. Nineteenth-century photographs and other archival material show how at harvest or haymaking – the two most important times in the farm calendar – the labourers would regularly quench their thirst with their part-wage payment of cider. The custom was that the cider was poured into a common drinking cup and handed round to each man in turn, going round in a circle, clockwise. This manner of sharing out the drink in turn using the same vessel seems an age-old custom or rite and is still found in some traditional cider-producing countries, for example at mealtimes around the table in such places as Asturias and Normandy. Indeed, in Asturias the meal itself cannot be commenced until each member has first drunk their small glass of cider, always to *Seventeenth-century milling machine*

9

be drunk down in one go – a sharing and kind of blessing, of labour and the harvest. Perhaps there are resonances here of something very old. Certainly, for a long time the apple tree itself was regarded as sacred, and possibly not just for the fact that it is a prime host for mistletoe.

There can be no doubt that cidermaking really grew up in those cooler north west regions of Europe where the vine finally gives way to the apple. Thus in northern Spain, Wiesbaden in Germany, Normandy and Brittany in France, and particularly the southern and western counties of England, the craft developed. In time, through emigration, the skills were exported to all those other temperate regions of the world in the northern and southern hemispheres where cider came to be made and is still appreciated today.

Although the first official references in England to cider come from royal accounts in the thirteenth century, cider has certainly been with us for a lot longer than that, predating the Romans, probably also the making of ale from barley and certainly beer.

While the fortunes of the drink seemed to have waxed and waned at the aristocrat's table, the tradition of making and drinking cider else-where in England and Wales where the apple thrived remained strong throughout the centuries. It appears to have reached its greatest popu-larity in the seventeenth and eighteenth centuries when it supplanted ale as the preferred drink. Among the upper classes some of the best 'keeved' ciders were compared to the finest French wines. John Evelyn published his great treatise, *Pomona*, on the subject of cider and all related subjects in 1670 and during the following centuries the publi-cations on orcharding and cidermaking tech-niques continued to flow, indicating just how important the drink had become. In fact, the popularity of the drink remained strong, even through difficult times in the nineteenth cen-tury, and has only declined substantially in the last fifty to sixty years. Each of the farms and those country estates with their own home farm and orchards would have had their cider mill and press, sometimes in their own building (the mill house), and the volumes of cider produced each year meant that they were usually more than self-sufficient in the drink.

Ye compleate smalle scale cydere maker

Chronicling the rich traditions surrounding every aspect of cider in Britain didn't really begin until our own century, and even then most has been accomplished since the Second World War. It draws upon a rich seam of archival material, mostly from the nineteenth century, corresponding to a time when the society slowly became more literate, increasingly industrialised (bringing profound changes to people's lives and customs) and saw the advent of such inventions as photography. In that century, and even up to the First World War and beyond, we discover the importance of cider to a rural agricultural society whcre it was made largely for consumption by the farm household and farm workers – so basic and unobtrusive a practice that it rarely even entered the farm accounts.

Technical changes, particularly the replacement of the wooden screw in the cider press by the first cast iron screws in the late eighteenth century, and the development of the much smaller scratter mill for the old horse-drawn mechanical means of crushing apples, produced another interesting scion of the tradition: the travelling cidermaker of the nineteenth century. He would travel about between farms that lay on the margins of the main apple-growing areas and which didn't have the means to support the necessary equipment, and also from inn to inn, in the short cidermaking season, extracting juice which the farmer and innkeeper would then ferment for the needs of workers or customers. The latest chapter in the story of cider really belongs to the growth of a few large manufacturers of cider. Towards the end of the nineteenth century, in response to the massive urbanisation occurring and a commensurate decrease in the numbers of agricultural labourers due to the scale of mechanisation, the needs and purposes behind the old farm-based tradition of making cider steadily began to die. The process continued well into the twentieth century, and saw perhaps another dramatic stage in decline with that great turning point in British society – the First World War. After that, while the tradition lingered on here and there, and even survived in isolated spots beyond the Second World War, to all intents and purposes the tradition was dead. And yet, perhaps we are already witnessing something of the proverbial phoenix. While it is certainly the factory-produced cider which dominates the market today, perhaps the renaissance of interest in real cider which has arisen in the last few years will, in the forms of the small-scale producer, and the 'domestic' and community production of cider come to represent the vigour of a new variety grafted onto the old stock.

4 Building the Press

It is said that after the First World War much of the farm cidermaking equipment was systematically bought up by a number of the growing commercial concerns. The farmers were only too pleased, for a little much needed cash, to get rid of equipment that was simply rusting and rotting way. Once purchased, the milling machines and presses were smashed up and burnt, so that they could never be used again.

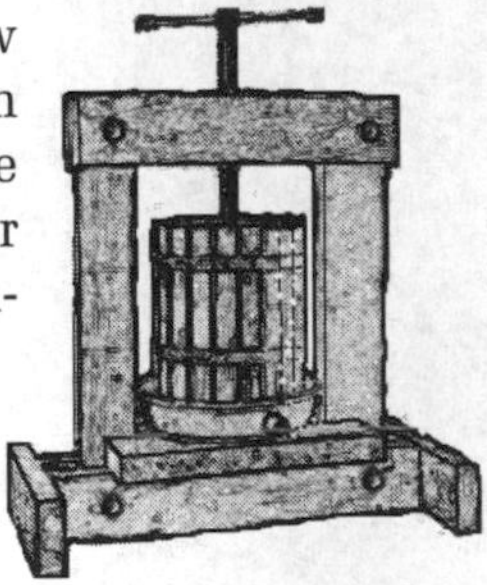

First comes the cider press. As George Borrow remarked: 'The effort in learning a foreign language is as nothing compared to the pleasure that follows from using it'. So it is with cider presses. Making the press – a simple and inexpensive matter – should be thought of as acquiring a piece of equipment as indispensable to the household or community in its way as, say, an oven, a radio, or a bicycle. The design of the press shown here is extremely sturdy, and based upon one type of traditional farm press. Once made, it will last a lifetime and beyond. It may even turn out to be a family heirloom! The press is a scaled down version of a simple single screw press comprising three main components:

- A heavy steel screw plunger mechanism obtained by mail order from a woodworking machinery supplier which requires some simple modification by any local metal working shop.

Pressing the apple pulp to juice.

- A bolted timber frame and base.
- A slatted box of approximately 10 litres capacity to contain the apple pulp and tray.

Some additional simple mild steel plates and stainless steel hoops are required but it is not difficult to find a small workshop which will do this for you fairly cheaply from information on the plans provided.

The finished press measures some 30 inches high by 24 inches wide and should give up to a third or half a gallon of juice to each pressing depending on how well the apples are pulped.

Full instructions for building your own press can be found at the end of this chapter on four illustrated sheets. For a consideration of other designs of presses suitable for producing much larger volumes of juice, see Chapter 9.

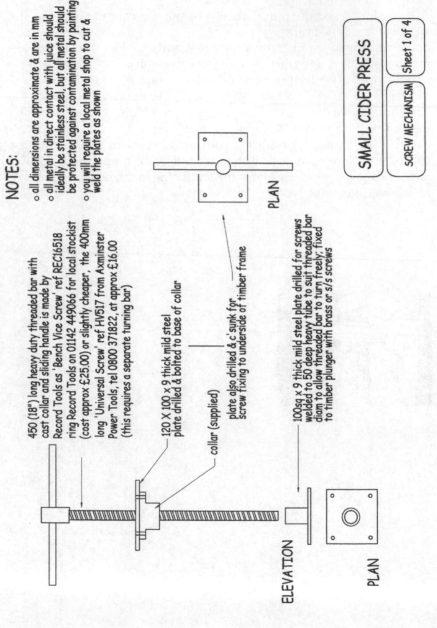

NOTES:

○ all dimensions are approximate & are in mm

○ all metal in direct contact with juice should ideally be stainless steel, but all metal should be protected against contamination by painting

○ you will require a local metal shop to cut & weld the plates as shown

450 (18") long heavy duty threaded bar with cast collar and sliding handle is made by Record Tools as 'Bench Vice Screw' ref REC16518 ring Record Tools on 01142 449066 for local stockist (cost approx £25.00) or slightly cheaper, the 400mm long 'Universal Screw' ref HV517 from Axminster Power Tools, tel 0800 371822, at approx £16.00 (this requires a separate turning bar)

120 X 100 x 9 thick mild steel plate drilled & bolted to base of collar

collar (supplied)

plate also drilled & c'sunk for screw fixing to underside of timber frame

100sq x 9 thick mild steel plate drilled for screws welded to 50 deep heavy tube to suit threaded bar diam to allow threaded bar to turn freely; fixed to timber plunger with brass or s/s screws

ELEVATION

PLAN

PLAN

SMALL CIDER PRESS

SCREW MECHANISM   Sheet 1 of 4

16

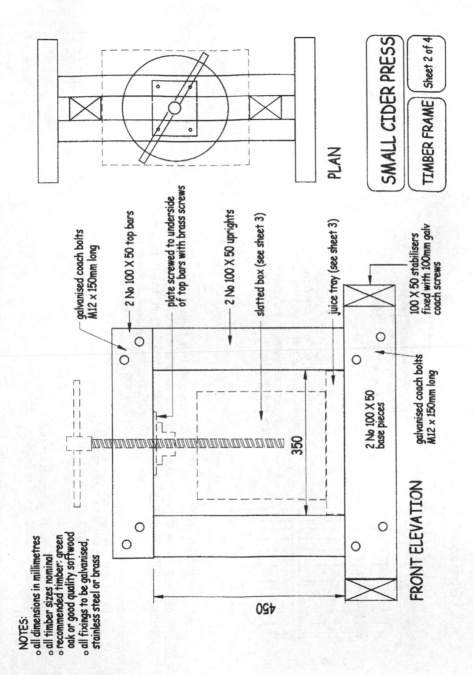

NOTES:
- all dimensions in millimetres
- all timber sizes nominal
- recommended timber: green oak or good quality softwood
- all fixings to be galvanised, stainless steel or brass

galvanised coach bolts M12 x 150mm long

2 No 100 X 50 top bars

plate screwed to underside of top bars with brass screws

2 No 100 X 50 uprights

slatted box (see sheet 3)

juice tray (see sheet 3)

100 X 50 stabilisers fixed with 100mm galv coach screws

2 No 100 X 50 base pieces

galvanised coach bolts M12 x 150mm long

350

450

PLAN

FRONT ELEVATION

SMALL CIDER PRESS

TIMBER FRAME | Sheet 2 of 4

17

18

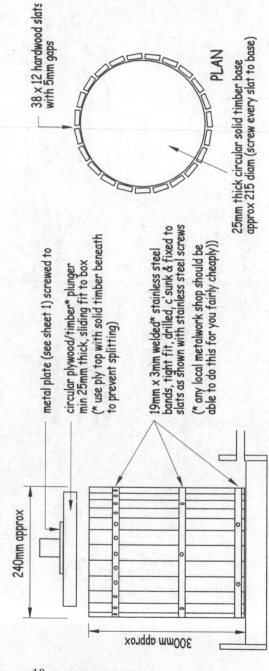

38 x 12 hardwood slats
with 5mm gaps

PLAN

25mm thick circular solid timber base
approx 215 diam (screw every slat to base)

240mm approx

300mm approx

FRONT ELEVATION

metal plate (see sheet 1) screwed to

circular plywood/timber* plunger
min 25mm thick, sliding fit to box
(* use ply top with solid timber beneath
to prevent splitting)

19mm x 3mm welded* stainless steel
bands, tight fit, drilled, c'sunk & fixed to
slats as shown with stainless steel screws

(* any local metalwork shop should be
able to do this for you fairly cheaply))

juice tray made from 40mm thick laminated worktop
offcut or similar with hardwood sides screwed and glued,
drilled for standard plastic hose pipe with spigot
OR plastic tray (eg large plant pot saucer max 350 dia)
on 40mm base

NOTES:

○ NB: the finer you can crush the apples
before pressing the greater the juice yield will be

○ all dimensions & sizes approximate only
○ cut out circular timber base & plunger first and construct
slatted container around them with metal hoops to tight fit
○ all metal in direct contact with apple juice should ideally
consist of stainless steel or similar to avoid tainting
○ use planed offcut oak for slats
○ use old nylon net curtain or similar as liner inside container
wrapped around pulp to strain juice (fill half to three quarters
for best results)

SMALL CIDER PRESS

SLATTED BOX   Sheet 3 of 4

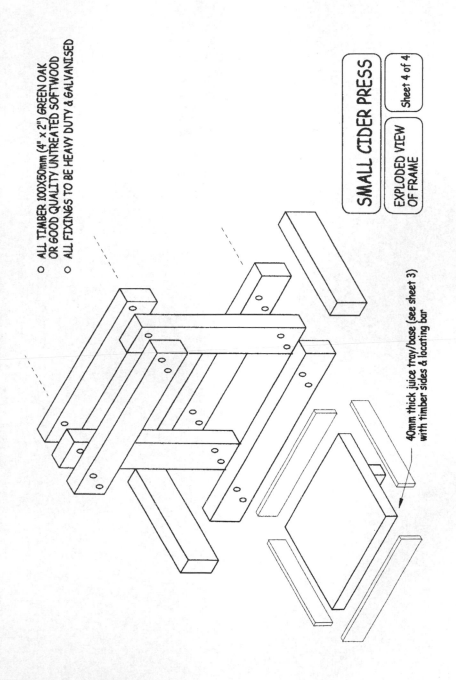

○ ALL TIMBER 100X50mm (4" x 2") GREEN OAK
   OR GOOD QUALITY UNTREATED SOFTWOOD
○ ALL FIXINGS TO BE HEAVY DUTY & GALVANISED

SMALL CIDER PRESS

EXPLODED VIEW
OF FRAME

Sheet 4 of 4

40mm thick juice tray/base (see sheet 3)
with timber sides & locating bar

5 An Autumn Day's Cidermaking

It's Pick & Mix
Wash & Chop
Crush & Press
Ferment . . . Store . . . Serve

S mall scale might mean producing anything from 1 to 2 gallons of cider up to a few hundred. Here the term is used to suggest a scale of cidermaking that employs only the most basic low-tech equipment, including the press.

Exactly how much juice is extracted in, say, a day of cidermaking will of course depend on the effort, but using such equipment roughly 20lb apples convert to a gallon of juice. In our experience 20 to 30 gallons of juice in a day would be considered very fair.

Those who would like to generate much larger quantities than this (perhaps thinking of retailing it) will necessarily have to secure a sufficient supply of apples, be prepared to set aside a number of days extracting the juice, and/or invest in larger, more sophisticated, equipment which is discussed in Chapter 9, *Pressing the Apple Pulp*. They will also need to be aware in Britain of the current excise duty on quantities of cider made for retail in excess of 7,000 litres. For some people the pleasure of a day or a season of making cider is a domestic or even individual affair, but cidermaking at this level, unlike beer and winemaking at home, is ideally a craft shared out among a group of people. Perhaps anywhere between half a dozen and a dozen people (with children, all the better) probably makes an ideal number, each bringing a contribution to the pile of apples, and at the end of the day taking away a share of the juice to be fermented at home. Clearly, if two or more presses are available then the larger numbers could work, for example at a small community day activity, but if the event is being hosted by an individual or a family they will need to be aware of keeping numbers manageable.

The most important aspect to the philosophy behind small-scale cidermaking is the celebration of the fact that it is low-tech and labour intensive. Therein lies its secret. The product is ultimately delicious and wholesome because at every stage it is completely touched by human hand! Unlike many modern commercial concoctions, which try to avoid, if at all possible, going anywhere near a human being (or an apple, for that matter!).

The pleasures and the satisfactions in making cider at this level lie as much in the diversity of the stages involved in getting the juice as the fermentation process to the final product. There is the gathering, mixing, washing, preparing and quartering of the apples with much banter across the table and intense discussions as to how the processes might be speeded up with better technology! There is a good deal of enjoyment to be had, not least by children, in the pounding of the quartered apples to crush them using a simple pole as a pestle (more sophisticated alternatives are available if preferred), and finally there is the satisfaction of the actual pressing, watching the apple juice come pouring out into its receptacle.

Tasting the juice is an experience in its own right, and to observe the reaction of the most ardent sceptic, who, after much urging from others, finally agrees to sample the thick muddy liquid, is as amusing as invariable. The face becomes suffused with astonishment and undisguised pleasure as to how delicious it is.

The whole process is of course extremely inefficient! At least, that

Completely touched by human hand! A day's cidermaking is labour-intensive and thoroughly enjoyable (irrespective of age).

is, if judged by the mean calculus of how much juice is extracted from how much time and energy is put in. But it is wonderfully efficient in terms of how much sharing takes place, how much fun is to be had, and efficient in the exercise, the wit and humour and gossip generated! As 'refreshing of the spirit' as the drinking of the cider will be in its own way in due course.

Choose, then, one of those lovely crisp sunny days in October, or even November, for your cidermaking day. A certain amount of planning will be necessary beforehand, but you will be blessed with fine weather anyway because cidermaking is a virtuous thing. If you are doing it communally, make certain people have had plenty of notice and are well-prepared. Food will be required (we normally arrange it that whoever is 'hosting' the event supplies lunch): extracting apple juice all day can build up a furious hunger. Drink, too, is completely indispensable, since what you are embarked upon is effectively a daylong party – a working party (of a different kind!) and thirsty work at that! Copious quantities of wine, beer, or even some of last year's cider (if you have any left) will help ensure that the wit and repartee and gossip begin to flow in line with the juice. Any questions of Puritan guilt about enjoying yourself too much may be safely discounted because you will be earning the enjoyment at a fair old rate of demi-johns and 5-gallon drums of pressed apple juice.

The equipment needed for small-scale cidermaking is simple:

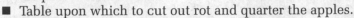

- The basket press with nylon sieve or square of net curtain or volume press with cloths and wooden racks for 'cheese' (see Chapter 9).
- Tub (eg plastic dustbin; avoid metal containers, except stainless steel) filled with water into which apples are poured and washed.
- Table upon which to cut out rot and quarter the apples.
- A couple of old 3–4 gallon plastic buckets for carrying apples to the table and for disposal of discarded apples.
- White, food grade 4–5 gallon plastic bucket/bin in which the quartered apples are crushed (see Chapter 8).
- A couple of 'pestle' poles (see Chapter 8).
- Simple scratting mill (optional: see Chapter 8).
- Fermentation vessels: glass demi-johns or white, food grade 5–6 gallon fermentation bins or anything else suitable.
- Sundries: cotton wool, cloths, fermentation locks, sodium metabisulphite etc.
- Large plastic dustbin or plastic dustbin liners into which is put the spent apple pulp (pomace) before composting etc.
- Access to an outside tap and, if possible, pressure hose for filling tubs and cleaning equipment at end of day.

Hard work watching the juice gushing out!

6 The Right Mix of Apples

First catch your apple.
Then another ...

Many potentially good ciders, and certainly a great deal of effort, are spoilt for want of having spent a bit of time at the outset in getting a balanced mix of apples. So often the would-be cidermaker simply gathers up what apples are there and gets straight into pounding and pressing. Understandable enough! This chapter, however, makes a simple plea to spend a little time in securing, if possible, a good mix of apples. The juice and the final product will reward handsomely the investment of the time.

There are great many varieties of genuine cider apples, some of long pedigree such as that most famous all-rounder, Kingston Black, along with the likes of Tom Putt, Foxwhelp and Brown Snout. And what of 'Slack Ma Girdle' for a name – an old sweet Devon variety perhaps alluding to cider's reputation for keeping you slim.

The variety is still available. Modern cultivars continue the tradition of both flavour and lovely names, such as Yarlington Mill, Dabinett and Chisel Jersey. Discussing the tradition of cider apples and the naming of apples could happily occupy another book in its own right.

Cider fruit

Cider fruit needs to be considered, however, to discover what makes a really good cider. Traditionally, such apples might very well have been eaten or used for cooking, but were often especially valued for making cider. They are most closely related to the wild crab apple, often appearing unattractively blotched and scabby, but having the characteristics in their juice that makes them excellent for cider. The juice has a sweetness and acidity, and a high level of tannin which imparts a bitterness and dryness in the mouth referred to as astringency. It is these three ingredients found in real cider apples which confer a range and complexity of flavours to the cider and which are at the heart of a really good cider.

Depending on the balance of tannin to sweetness or acidity, cider apples are generally divided into two categories: *bittersweets* and *bittersharps*. These days *bittersweets* are the preferred type of cider apples used most often commercially in Britain. *Sweets* and *sharps* are two further low-tannin categories used in describing cider fruit. All other apples which are not typified as cider varieties – but which can still be used to make cider – are referred to as dessert apples ('eaters') culinary apples ('cookers') and those that are dual purpose. The table below gives the compositions of some typical apple juices along with a target or ideal juice composition for the making of excellent ciders.

Consideration of these values leads us to a further interesting characteristic of some cider fruit which is more than noteworthy. Those cultivars which are regarded as producing the very finest ciders in

The composition of some apple juices. Approximate % values expressed as mass (g)/100ml of juice.

Property	Typical pure sweet	Typical pure sharp	Typical bittersweet	Juice target for excellent ciders
Sugar	13	11	15	15
Malic acid	0.2	1	0.2	0.4
Tannin	0.15	0.15	0.3	0.2

terms of body and flavour are known as vintage quality. The term is difficult to define precisely in biochemical terms, but just as with varieties of grapes or hops or barley there are some apple cultivars that possess superior attributes of sugar, acid, tannin and a host of other subtle qualities that affects the rate and nature of the fermentation and therefore the quality of the resultant cider. Compared to the great number of (still available) cider apple varieties, the number of vintage examples are relatively few, but in cidermaking circles there appears to be a general consensus as to those cultivars that have vintage quality. Some of the more important examples with their characteristics are listed below.

Vintage cider cultivars

Cultivar	Category	Cider characteristics
Browns Apple	Pure sharp	Light, sharp and fruity cider
Fair Maid of Devon	Pure sharp	Excellent juice volume; sharp and fruity cider
Kingston Black	Medium bittersweet	Full-bodied, spicy, regarded the finest vintage variety
Stoke Red	Medium bittersweet	Full-bodied, fruity, excellent single variety cider
Broxwood Foxwhelp	Medium bittersweet	Full-bodied, very distinctive aroma and flavour
Ashton Brown Jersey	Full bittersweet	Good quality, astringent cider
Sercombes Natural	Mild bittersweet	Soft tannin cider
Somerset Redstreak	Mild bittersweet	Good body, soft tannin cider, useful blender
Dabinett	Full bittersweet	Full-bodied, soft tannin, indispensable for blending
Yarlington Mill	Mild bittersweet	Good body, fruity, soft tannin, superior cider
Major	Full bittersweet	Fruity, average quality, useful for blending
Harry Masters Jersey	Medium bittersweet	Soft astringent tannin, very good single varietal cider
Medaille D'Or	Full bittersweet	High levels of soft tannin, good quality cider
Sweet Coppin	Pure sweet	Very useful vintage cider
Sweet Alford	Pure sweet	One of the most valuable all-round vintage ciders

At a small scale or domestic level, most people will, of course, simply use whatever apples are to hand; this is as it should be. Any and all apples will do! Early or late windfalls, apples shaken down, hand-picked, begged, borrowed. However, the best apples to use are the ripest ones, since these will have the highest sugar contents and produce the richest and most alcoholic ciders.

Apples will begin to fall in September and are best piled up, say, on a plastic sheet, or better still sacking, on the ground, grass, or orchard floor, over the coming weeks until you choose the opportune day to commence cidermaking. Cover the top of the pile with old carpet or sacking to protect it from the worst of the weather. In the pile the apples will continue to ripen, soften, and begin to smell very sweet. Add to it from whatever source. If the main bulk of the apples are from late maturing sources, then you will obviously be choosing a day in November to make cider, but everything else being equal, October is really the month for it. It has a further advantage, alluded to more than once in this book that, if fermented a little faster, then bottled or otherwise stored, the cider will be ready by Christmas and a glass of chilled cider in a house sometimes singing with the warmth of Christmas preparations, or an offering of mulled cider when coming in from a frosted evening of carols are pleasures indeed!

If your pile, or tump, of apples is likely to be left for some time, it is advisable at periodic intervals to turn it over, removing those apples that are brown rotten due to the *botrytis* fungus. The rate of infection of sound apples can be very rapid (see Appendix 3).

We can aspire to as rich and balanced a juice as possible by considering for a moment what is involved. Learn to recognise the culinary type such as the Bramley or other green 'cookers' which are rich in acid, and the dessert apple or 'eaters' which will be relatively sweet.

You may also have access to apples which, upon tasting, demonstrate a fair degree of astringency. If this is appears to be lacking from all of your apples, **add a small ration of crab apples to the mix** to supply the tannin. Try to aim for a mix of these types and spend a few minutes physically mixing them up before cleaning and chopping and preparing the apple pulp prior to pressing. If you are uncertain at the apple mixing-up stage whether you have got the right balance, then wait until you've pressed out some juice and taste it. It will always be delicious, but if it is demonstrably sweet while lacking distinctive acidity on the palate, then you will need to add more 'cookers' to the mix as you go along.

You can adjust an over-acid juice by piling in more of the dessert apples with the next press. Try to avoid a preponderance of cooking apples in the mix; this is because once the apple sugars have been fermented to alcohol, the acidity will be a very dominant feature of the resulting cider, and this may even experience more difficulty in clearing.

Blending juices

An alternative to blending the fruit prior to pressing is for the cidermaker to press individual cultivars, assess the nature of the resultant juice from each, and then blend to arrive at the desired balanced juice before fermentation (there may or may not be a need to make further adjustments to the juice as discussed in Chapter 9). Many cidermakers operate this way, arguing that they have greater control over the blending process in consequence. If you intend following this procedure, clearly you will need to keep your fruit in separate piles. One of the great advantages of this approach is that you will certainly get to know the characteristics of your individual cider cultivars and their juices.

Blending ciders

It is even the case that a great many cidermakers (especially those retailing cider) do not even bother to blend either fruit or juice at this stage. Instead, they press and ferment single varietal ciders and leave any necessary blending to the final cider stage. Once again, this is an excellent opportunity to relate the individual cultivar to its cider characteristics and you may wish to adopt this approach. However, in general, if you are a relative beginner to the craft, it is probably advisable to blend at the fruit or juice stage and leave cider blending itself until you have gained more experience. Blending ciders is considered much more fully in Chapter 11.

Conclusion

The following example will illustrate the main thrust of this chapter. Recently, we tasted a dry still cider made, as it turned out, from 21 different varieties of cidermaking apples – many of them venerable indeed, and all with the most delicious of names printed on a splendid label. The product, alas, was bland and hugely disappointing! Why? Almost certainly because of a basic failure to establish a sound blend, a balance between the contrasting types of apple that make a really good cider. In the same way, although the products are much vaunted, many people find the fashion for 'single varietal' ciders disappointing. Apart from notable exceptions, such as the Kingston Black, or other bittersweet vintage cider apples, many single varieties will tend to produce a cider with none of the heady aroma, the full flavour of luscious apples, and all those other subtleties and nuances which should be the feature of a traditional cider. As with people, so with apples for cider – the more contrasting types you have together, the richer the event!

7 Washing and Preparing the Apples

When you have chosen cidermaking day (or even days!) and are ready to press the fruit, gather it to the site, discard all fruit that is in any way mouldy or excessively bruised (see Appendix 6) and then, if you haven't done it already, try to establish a good blend of the

different apples you have, according to the principles set out in the previous chapter. (Alternatively, you may wish to treat the preparation and subsequent pressing of the apples on a 'single variety' basis.)

Pour the apples in batches into a large bucket or tub of cold water and give them a thorough wash around, removing soil, bloom, surface sliminess and any rotten apples which will usually sink. It is important to wash the apples thoroughly at this stage to

Cutting out rot and quartering apples prior to milling or crushing them.

remove any enteric bacteria such as those originating, say, from animal-grazed orchards, and also to minimise those wild yeasts on the skin which may contribute to cider taint such as 'mousiness' (see Chapter 12, *Troubleshooting*).

Change the water at periodic intervals, or use a hose to fill up with fresh water. Transfer the cleaned apples to a table where they should be quartered. Cut out the worst of any rot and bruising, but do not be over fastidious or attempt to remove cores and pips as some beginning the craft believe is necessary! As any child knows who has ever bitten on a pip and explored it, there is a range of delicious flavours to be experienced. It was this that the old cidermakers, using a mechanical means of crushing and pulverising the apple prior to pressing, regarded as adding another distinctive dimension to the flavour of the final cider, and which they asserted was much reduced with the development of the scratting mill.

Apart from these obvious preliminaries, you can use the apples as they come and this stage should be done relatively quickly and without in any way being onerous.

8 Milling and Crushing the Apples

The pressure required to extract even a fraction of the juice from a whole apple is remarkable. For this reason it is necessary to mill and/or crush the apples beforehand; the more completely this is done, the more juice will be extracted when pressing. Be aware that in a particularly dry year, when the apples may have far less juice in them than normal, that as well as the need for softening in the stacked pile prior to pressing, you will need to crush the quartered apples that bit more thoroughly to extract as much juice as possible.

There are commercially available devices known as scratters or scratting mills (a type of mincer) operated by hand (or by electricity) and if you find cidermaking to your taste in a big way, you may wish to invest in a small domestic example. Some people make good use of

'Double bashing' of quartered apples. Low-tech but all the more skill to keep in step!

Milling the quartered apples with a small hand-operated scratter (mind fingers!).

garden shredders for the purpose of milling apples! However, for most people the easiest – and by far the cheapest – approach to arriving at the apple pulp is to physically crush the quartered apples using a 2m length of timber, approximately 10–12cm square, or if you have access to woodland, a pole of any timber of similar diameter. If you want to make this even more efficient, drill laterally through the pole 6–8cm from the top and insert a short length of 25mm dowel to provide a handle on either side. Insert another handle(s) lower down if you want to be thoroughly child-friendly!

Now place about a 20cm depth of quartered apples in a food grade plastic bucket (white or clear is best, avoid highly coloured) or a wooden pail, and pulverise with the pole. Make sure you place the plastic bucket on a flat, level piece of ground, free of protruding stones to avoid splitting the base of the bucket as you bash. Stainless steel vessels could also be used, but otherwise avoid any metal container since apple juice is an acidic liquid which both attacks and is tainted by, metal.

With two people operating the pole on either side of each other this is known as a 'double-splodge' or 'double-bash' and builds up to a rhythmic pounding similar to the work of pounding maize and other cereals in the Third World. Indeed, in the best sense of the word, there is something primitive and peculiarly satisfying, especially for the child in us, in operating one of these poles. Comparisons have also shown that although extremely low-tech, at this level the pole is as efficient at getting the apple into the requisite state for pressing as the small scratting mill (although even if using this, the milled apple should be pounded somewhat afterwards anyway). The apple pulp should be nice and sloppy! It will also benefit in flavour from the fact that many of the pips have become crushed.

On an historical and recreational note, you may, if you feel so inclined, develop songs to accompany the pounding and bashing of the apples. As in the best tradition of repetitive rhythmic physical work (sailors with their sea shanties, for example) songs aid the labour and undoubtedly extract more juice (probably in trying to remember the words, you forget what you are doing!). At least, it is another opportunity to sing, and then there is the sense of feeling connections, actually physically living a part of a long tradition. Almost certainly, before the horse-drawn stone mill wheel entered the scene (let alone the scratting mill), our earliest medieval forebears would have used the same sort of poles or pounding devices. To be doing precisely the same thing now as a part of the same craft of cidermaking is to be rather more than just historically in touch with those ancestors and a little part of their lives across the hundreds of intervening years.

9 Pressing the Apple Pulp

"I remember we didn't have a press for two or three years. You get desperate, don't you? We used the spin cycle of the automatic washing machine, putting the apple pulp in a pillow case and producing batches of 20–30 gallons of juice without any difficulty. Mind you, we made sure the pipes were well clear of soap beforehand!"

It is amazing the length some cidermakers will go to get their juice! If using a small basket press, however, of the type built in Chapter 4, set it up at a convenient height so that you don't have to bend much at all. Inside the slatted box you will need to fit a nylon sieve bag or a large square of nylon net curtain which is then folded over the pulp. You should avoid net curtain in which the weave is either too large or too fine but otherwise, any will do, and provided it is washed out and dried at the end of the cidermaking session(s), will give good service for years.

Load up the sieve bag or net curtain, previously placed on the inside of the basket, by scooping up apple pulp (best and stickiest by hand) between half and two-thirds full for maximum extraction of juice. Turn the thread, making sure you engage it in the press plate on top of the pulp: the juice runs out between the slats into the

collection tray and thence, by means of a funnel or length of plastic hose, into a suitable container. It is most convenient to press this juice directly into the fermentation container(s), either glass demi-johns or 5–6 gallon food grade plastic fermentation bins that can take a fermentation lock. Make certain that the vessels are thoroughly clean before allowing the apple juice to run into them (see *Preparing the fermentation vessels* in Chapter 10).

Operating at higher volumes of juice/cider (50 gallons upwards)

If you have access to larger supplies of fruit – plentiful farm fruit or from your own planted orchard perhaps – you may be intending to produce much higher volumes of cider than are practically possible with the basket press described so far. You will need to build or purchase a press whose design and capacity reflect your ambitions. There are a number of different types available from commercial suppliers, or even from farms where an old press might have lain abandoned for years and can be bought cheaply enough. This is particularly true in Normandy and Brittany where there are many good presses to be had that have remained in farm outbuildings or dedicated ciderhouses for years; it is simply a question of getting to know of their existence. Advertise in the local press if necessary. Usually, once it is known you are looking for a press, word gets round and someone somewhere will point you in the right direction.

One common type of larger volume press uses a central screw with a ratchet and arm mechanism; this is a relatively simple design and easy to operate. Harder work, but even sturdier in the long run, is the twin-screw press with the head block (a beam of oak usually) supported in collars which fit into special grooves in the nuts used to screw the head block down onto the pulp below. Each nut has three or four fixed wrought 'wings' which are first turned by hand, each screw alternately, and when the going gets tough by a lever arm. A third class of press can

Action-packed exercise – no wonder the juice and cider taste so good!

be made very simply using a hydraulic car jack, nothing more actually being needed than a fixed beam or joist above and against which the jack can push.

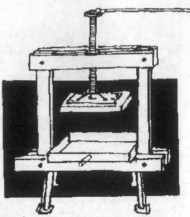

However, all of these types of press require that the apple pulp is piled up underneath – no mean feat given that it is far too sloppy to stay in one place. The technique is to 'bind up' the pulp in some way. Traditionally, this was done by mixing pulp with straw to make what was called a 'mock'. More commonly, the pulp was carefully folded into a medium sized mesh sacking or cloths known as 'hairs' and built up to make a 'cheese'. The term is still used nowadays and in operating these larger presses every cidermaker takes pleasure in building up the cheese or 'rack' – an absolutely essential stage in the craft prior to obtaining the juice. Straw and sacking have long been replaced by terylene or other polyester cloths which are filled with a few centimetres of apple pulp before each cloth is carefully folded over and separated by good hardwood, semi-hardwood or plastic racks until the cheese is built up.

The final stage requires placing a heavy board on top of the cheese to spread the weight, before applying initially gentle pressure to control the flood of juice. The height of each cheese depends, of course, on the type of press being used and therefore the pressure capable of being applied, half a dozen layers of pulp being a typical quantity to press at any one go for a medium-sized press.

This arrangement provides very good drainage channels for the

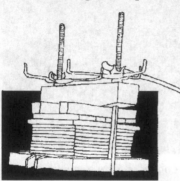

juice (just as traditional set-ups did) which is collected in the tray or trough at the base of the press, made of hardwood timber, synthetic materials, or traditional stone – all materials unsusceptible to attack by apple juice.

Whichever press you use, the juice will come pouring out with a distinctly muddy appearance, due to the almost immediate onset of oxidation of tannins. This is perfectly normal but the cider you make will be a beautiful clear(ish) golden colour. Remember to taste the juice as you go along and, if possible, adjust for sweetness, acidity and tannin by pressing more of the appropriate apples. If, however, you have only one type of apple at your disposal and you feel that the balance is wrong, or the juice is insipid, there are one or two additives you can use from the winemaker's cupboard to arrive at a better balance before you embark

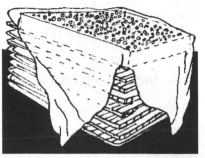

Building up the 'cheese' or 'rack' with layers of cloth-wrapped apple pulp separated by wooden or plastic racks

upon the fermentation discussed in Chapter 10. Obviously, this will depend on how you feel about additives in general, but it has to be said that an insipid juice will give a very poor cider and to correct the problem at this point is much better than gross disappointment later!

Adjusting the balance of acidity

To adjust for lack of acidity, make up a small concentrated solution of preferably malic acid (if available), citric acid, tartaric acid, or a mixture of these in as small a volume of very hot water as possible. Now add a little of this solution to a specimen gallon of juice. Shake thoroughly to distribute evenly, taste and if necessary add a little more acid. See how the overall quality of the juice is immediately improved *but do not overdo the acid*! Make a note of the total volume of acid you added to the gallon demi-john, then add on a pro-rata basis to 5–6 gallon quantities if you are working with these volumes.

To adjust for over acidity, you can use either precipitated chalk or, better still, potassium carbonate (whose neutralisation products leave no taste) by thoroughly dissolving a little in the juice, incrementally, tasting once again as you go. Frankly, this problem will only arise if you are endeavouring to make cider with far too high a preponderance of culinary fruit.

You may wish to be more scientific in your estimation of the juice's level of acidity by investing in what have become relatively cheap electronic pH meters. You are aiming for a juice whose pH is somewhere in the region 3.2 to 3.8. Avoid the use of garden pH meters or pH papers or solution which are far too inaccurate to be of any use to us here.

Adjusting the balance of tannin

To adjust for poor tannin levels, add and thoroughly dissolve a pinch of winemaker's tannin to each gallon of juice, and as much as half a level teaspoon of tannin per 5–6 gallon quantity of juice. Alternatively, you can add up to 1 tablespoon of strong tea as a source of tannin per gallon of juice. Juices that make the mouth pucker severely are likely to have too much tannin in them and this can be reduced by adding a little proprietary gelatine finings. Dissolve a little of this in hot water and then add on a trial basis to establish its efficacy: the tannin will be thrown out of solution but don't worry about filtering at this stage.

Adding pectolytic enzyme to the juice

Fresh well-balanced juice made in the autumn from the current crop of apples is unlikely to require the addition of pectic or pectolytic enzyme since it has sufficient concentration of its own natural enzyme. If this is the case, the general advice is not to bother with this addition. Juices, however, that are derived from a high proportion of dessert apples or/and from relatively long-stored fruit will benefit from the addition of the enzyme as a pre-emptive strike against the possibility of haze in the final cider. Pectin is a natural carbohydrate found in all apples (and many other fruits) and when released during fermentation can be precipitated by the developing alcohol to produce a characteristic pectin haze. The usual recommended dosage is 1 tablespoon of the enzyme per gallon of juice, making certain it is well dissolved.

Making any of these adjustments of acid, tannin and pectolytic enzyme may very well be worth considering and are recommended if you feel the juice warrants them. You could experiment with a single gallon of juice, label the final cider clearly to distinguish it from the rest, and then determine whether the taste and character have justified the extra solicitations.

Increasing sweetness in the pressed juice

Any lack of sweetness in the pressed juice (and therefore the ultimate alcoholic strength of the cider) is probably best adjusted for at the first racking stage as discussed in Chapter 10. This gives the opportunity for the young cider to be taken off the lees and, providing the ambient temperature is warm enough, will not slow the process down at all. However, if fermenting at much larger volumes, say, in barrels (9 gallons, 36 gallons etc.), it is recommended that you adjust the sweetness at this pressed juice stage to avoid the need for an earlier racking. Add white sugar as a syrup to the juice. Make up the syrup by adding a measured weight of white sugar to a pan with the minimum of water needed to produce a clear syrup upon gentle boiling. Allow this to cool before adding.

You will need first to measure the specific gravity (SG) of the juice and then add the sugar (syrup) per gallon at the rate indicated by the hydrometer to bring it to the preferred ultimate alcoholic strength. See text sections on specific gravity and Appendix 4, *Using the Hydrometer*. You can, of course, substitute glucose syrup, or, if you have no problems with it, apple juice concentrate as alternatives to white sugar. You will need to make your own calculations regarding strength. Alternatively, you may incline to a purist point of view and be opposed to the addition of any sweetening agent, in which case you will proceed with fermentation to make a dry cider or/and refer to Chapter 10.

Spent pressed apple cake

Pomace is the term used for apple pulp either before or after juice extraction. The spent pressed apple cake should be put in a large container or plastic dustbin bag as you proceed. There were examples traditionally of small quantities of water being added to it and a second pressing undertaken but in our experience the amount and quality of the resulting juice simply doesn't justify the time or effort. The spent apple or pomace was often fed to the pig along with its other delicacies of stale bread, potato peelings, and those wild flowers and dandelions hand-picked by the children. If you haven't got a pig, chickens love it! If you haven't got chickens, compost it, layering it between the other kitchen waste and composting material.

Finally, remember, after your cidermaking sessions, or each time you use the equipment to thoroughly wash it in cold water, removing all traces of juice and milled apple. A high pressure hose can be particularly useful. Leave the equipment to thoroughly dry then store. When you come to it again, perhaps after a year's absence, it should, after a quick swill round with cold water or a little sterilising fluid (rinsed off), be sweet and ready for use again.

10 Fermentation

Ye wolle obferve a greate agitafion at the ope of the barrelle. Some faye yt is the werme at werke, otheres the scavengyng beetle bringes forthe the cydere.

Once pressed, the apple juice is ready to be fermented and should be started without delay. From now on, the techniques you use will decide what kind of cider you finally get to drink. Assuming you started off with a balanced mix of apples, or adjusted juice, the cider will always be delicious, but you will have to decide what type is to your preference. Still or naturally conditioned? Artificially conditioned? Completely dry, medium dry, medium sweet, or even sweet cider? All of these are possible and this chapter is devoted to the approaches needed to arrive at any of the above ciders, still or conditioned.

It is also worth mentioning, that not everyone's taste, say, within a family, is the same; it seems a pity that for want of a little flexibility and readiness to experiment to make different ciders, some members of the family or wider circle are excluded from enjoying the final product.

Transferring the pressed juice from a glass demi-john to a 5-gallon food grade plastic drum for bulk fermentation.

Preparing the fermentation vessels

If you haven't pressed the juice actually into fermenting vessels, you should transfer it either into glass demi-johns or food grade (preferably white, avoid highly-coloured) 5–6 gallon plastic fermentation drums that can take a rubber bung/cork and fermentation lock. Any other suitable glass or plastic vessels can be used (eg old Winchesters, sherry containers, or acid carboys, provided they are strictly clean and smell 'sweet'); similarly, wooden vessels such as old oak casks or barrels can be used if available, but not metal barrels, with the exception of food grade stainless steel (this is very expensive). Never use anything smelling musty. The strictures regarding cleanliness and smelling 'sweet' apply to any vessel the apple juice or cider comes into contact with, including the bottles you may eventually use to store the finished product. Avoid any other metal container. Remember, apple juice and cider are both acidic and can easily taint.

Make certain the vessels are thoroughly clean and washed out with cold water, then use a little sterilising fluid. Swill round with a tiny amount of proprietary fluid, or one or two Campden tablets crushed and dissolved in a little water, or half a teaspoon of sodium metabisulphite crystals with a pinch of citric acid in a little water. All of these exploit the toxicity of sulphur dioxide to micro-organisms (and to higher forms of life in sufficient concentration) which has been used since medieval times and is now found in the hydrogensulphite form in a great many retailed foodstuffs and drinks. Remember, when using sterilising chemicals, *always to work in a well ventilated area*, since you are dealing with irritants.

When sterilising, make certain that immediately afterwards you rinse out well with cold water to remove traces of the sulphur dioxide or other chemicals (which might otherwise inhibit or even kill the culturing yeast used to ferment the juice in the fermentation stage).

The question of sulphiting juice prior to fermentation

One Campden tablet will provide the equivalent of 50 ppm (parts per million) of sulphur dioxide dissolved in 1 gallon of liquid. Other sources of sulphur dioxide have already been referred to.

Some cidermakers and other commentators recommend adding up to 2 Campden tablets per gallon of juice prior to fermentation on the grounds of suppressing wild yeasts and bacteria in the juice that may contribute to the possibility of spoilage. Once again, whether you follow this advice will depend on the nature of the juice you have produced and your general attitude towards additives of this kind. Two things are clear. First, purists abhor the use of sulphur dioxide and insist with some justification that providing the juice is fresh and well balanced, that the equipment is scrupulously clean and that the culturing *Saccharomyces* yeast (either natural or added) is in sufficient concentration (if being added, that it is done so as soon after the juice is pressed as practicable), there is simply no need ever to be involved with Campden tablets or other sources of sulphur dioxide. Secondly, it is also true that sometimes the above criteria are not met, in which case there is some evidence to suggest that adding Campden tablets to the juice can help. There can be no doubt that juices that are insipid, having too little acidity (pH values above 3.8) are prone to microbial infection due to native microbes in the juice and that adding Campden tablets can inhibit their growth, while at the same time allowing a much higher concentration of existent desirable *Saccharomyces* yeasts to continue to grow. The question nevertheless has to be asked: why is an insipid, acid-deficient juice being made in the first place?

The crux of the situation is whether the desirable *Saccharomyces* yeasts **are** in sufficient concentration in the juice since sulphur dioxide is also toxic to these and not just to the undesirables! If the level of these yeasts is also initially low (eg in juices that it is intended should be fermented without adding a wine yeast – see next section), then adding Campden tablets/sulphiting at this stage could inhibit successful fermentation altogether. The point is that even if undesirable microbes in the juice have been suppressed by sulphur dioxide, unless the fermentation gets off to a galloping start, quickly leading to a blanket of 'sterile' carbon dioxide above the juice, other sets of airborne yeasts and bacteria will quickly move in to spoil the juice anyway. Such is the nature of microbiology! Having said all this, there are many cidermakers who do sulphite especially to destroy wild *Brettanomyces* yeasts which are found in some juices and are held responsible for the formation of a very unpleasant condition known as 'mouse taint'. If you've suffered from this problem, the remedy is available in sulphiting.

In 20 years of cidermaking we have never actually had the need to use Campden tablets in the juice, but then we've always been able to follow the code below:

- Always use thoroughly washed and sound fruit, preferably recently gathered
- Never make an insipid, acid-deficient juice.
- If you do make an insipid, acid-deficient juice, always correct at least this acid imbalance prior to fermentation as described earlier.
- Make sure the nutrient nitrogen and phosphorus levels are adequate, and that the juice is in a warm enough place – at least initially for the *Saccharomyces* yeast to get the fermentation underway quickly.

If you cannot follow this code for whatever reason, or if you are of a particularly nervous disposition, then by all means sulphite with 1 Campden tablet per gallon of juice, but if intending pitching with a proprietary wine yeast as described below, *do not do so until at least 24–36 hours have elapsed after having treated the juice with Campden tablets or metabisulphite*. This is to allow time for the free sulphur dioxide to have 'discharged itself' by killing the low levels of spoilage organisms, and thus minimising the chances of damaging the culturing yeast you intend adding.

Fermenting the juice

Traditionally, nothing was added to the juice; naturally occurring yeasts present in the air, or persisting from season to season on the equipment in the ciderhouse would simply convert the sugars in the juice into alcohol, ie to produce the cider. It is now known that very little of the wild *Saccharomyces* ('sugar fungus') yeasts responsible for fermentation actually exist within the fruit itself; other wild yeasts do but these are more a source of trouble than help. The obvious signs of fermentation taking place were a vigorous frothing at the mouth of the cask

or barrel which would occur within a day or two of pressing, or a little longer if the temperature was colder. You may wish to follow this traditional method and there are many modern cidermakers who do so successfully all the time. Indeed, they regard it as a virtue, claim that the product is superior as a consequence, and generally adopt a laudable purist line in their craft. *A word of caution, however*! Nine times out of ten, apple juice under normal circumstances will begin to naturally ferment. But occasionally – because of low temperature, insufficient concentration of wild *Saccharomyces* yeasts or their nutrients in the juice, or for other indeterminate reasons – the fermentation is sluggish or refuses to get going. If this state of affairs continues for more than a day or two, the juice by contact with air will quickly begin to spoil, turn sour and become unusable. It will be lost.

For this reason it is recommended you use a fresh good quality proprietary dried wine yeast (eg usually varieties of *Saccharomyces cerevisae* or *banyanus*) which has with it added yeast nutrients. These are usually of the ammonium phosphate type or other sources of nitrogen and phosphorus to ensure rapid and reliable growth of the yeast. The other advantage to adding a wine yeast of this type is that it will be relatively high-alcohol tolerant, giving the cidermaker a greater flexibility over the final product. *Baker's or brewer's yeasts should not be used.*

As soon as possible, therefore, after the juice has been pressed, add a couple of teaspoons of dried yeast compound to each gallon demijohn, swirl round, put in a loose sterile cotton wool plug for the first few days, place on a piece of newspaper, and leave in a warmish place such as a kitchen. For 5–6 gallon quantities of juice, 4 teaspoons of yeast compound are sufficient. For even larger volume containers, add yeast on a pro-rata basis.

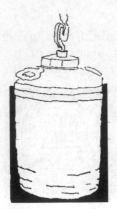

A convenient 6–7 gallon plastic fermenter

Within a day or two of adding the yeast (or without if adopting the traditional method) it should be obvious that the fermentation is well under way by the brown 'debris' that emerges from the top of the demi-john, often lifting off the loose cotton wool plug, and running down onto the newspaper below. This will continue for a couple of days or so before the fermentation relaxes and settles down. At this stage use a cotton wool swab soaked in warm water to clean the inside neck of the demi-john (and the outside) and fit a fermentation lock, which allows the carbon dioxide to escape, while preventing the entry of air. Top up with cold water to replace lost juice to within 2–3cm of the base of the bung.

From now on leave it in the kitchen if you have space or put it in a place where the ambient temperature is a normal room temperature of about 60°F or 15°C. The juice will, however, ferment at much lower temperatures than this if necessary. If you want to start drinking the final cider sooner rather than later, at Christmas/New Year for example, you can ferment at a higher temperature up to, say, 70°F or 21°C, but don't go beyond this range of temperatures (see Chapter 12, *Troubleshooting*).

If you can't, or don't want to fast ferment, that's fine. Providing the initial fermentation has got underway, and that it isn't subsequently too cold, the fermentation will just proceed that much more slowly. It is advisable, however, not to allow the fermenting juice to ever get so cold that the fermentation stops or becomes 'stuck', since once that happens and remains for any period of time the possibility of the juice spoiling increases considerably. It is the constant production of carbon dioxide by the fermentation process that effectively keeps the juice from spoiling and makes certain that you always have control over the process.

Similarly, try to avoid sharp fluctuations in the ambient temperature, since the received wisdom is that a smooth fermentation produces a better product. The amount of sugar in the apple juice before fermentation begins will, if entirely converted, determine the level of alcohol in the final cider. A hydrometer indicates **approximately** the sugar content through measuring the specific gravity (SG) of the juice. In the unfermented pressed juice the specific gravity (sometimes referred to as the original gravity or OG) is likely to be between SG 1035 and 1060, depending on the overall 'sweetness' of the mix of apples you used to arrive at the juice. The table indicates the maximum alcohol potential if all the sugars are converted.

It can be seen that a 5 degree rise in specific gravity attributed to sugar

Specific gravity (SG)	Alcohol by volume (ABV)
1035	3.7
1040	4.3
1045	5.2
1050	6.1
1055	7.0
1060	7.8
1065	8.5
1070	9.3

results in an approximate rise in alcohol by volume of 0.6 to 0.8% depending on the SG. If you want to know what potential alcohol could result just from the sugars in your juice, if completely converted, you will need to take a specific gravity reading before fermentation is started and consult the above table (see Appendix 4 for further discussion on the use of the hydrometer).

The yeast will continue to ferment the juice until the point is reached that either the sugars have been exhausted or the alcohol level has risen to the limit of the tolerance of the yeast. Whichever of these two factors is arrived at earlier will determine when the fermentation ceases. For the juice to ferment out completely can take anywhere between a fortnight to several weeks or even months, depending upon the temperature and original sweetness of the juice.

When we begin to approach the end of this first stage of fermentation it will be time to rack the cider.

Racking

Racking is the term used when syphoning off the completely or largely fermented out juice from the apple lees and yeast deposit at the bottom of the fermentation vessel. It can also be used as a technique to remove the still sweet cider from the lees before all the sugar has been consumed: see traditionalist/purist position below on making medium dry/medium sweet/sweet ciders without adding sugar. It is an extremely useful and important technique which, apart from helping to stabilise and clear the cider, and reduce potential off-flavours from the dying yeast (autolysis), will be used as the starting point for the actual cider you want.

The point at which this first racking should take place is when the fermentation has very nearly ceased, as indicated by the extremely slow passage of bubbles through the lock, and by observing that the young cider is slightly murky, with a good bed of yeast and lees. Alternatively, or as well as, a hydrometer can be used. This will register a reading of about 1005 or below, indicating that almost all the sugars have been converted.

When this point is reached, syphon off the cider from the lees and yeast deposit by first tying a syphon tube 2cm (or a little more if necessary) from the end of a clean cane and inserting the arrangement down to the bottom of the fermentation vessel. Alternatively, there are available 'shepherd-crook' syphoning devices which avoid the lees.

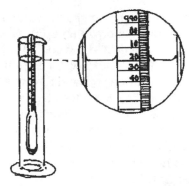

Rack into another clean vessel of a similar capacity, top up with cold water and proceed to the next stage. If, however, you are not doing this

The correct reading here is 1020 (not 1015)

because sugar was already added at the juice stage, go to the section 'Making different still ciders'. If you hold a purist belief against adding sugar, go to the section on 'Making medium dry, medium sweet and sweet ciders by traditional techniques *without adding sugar*'.

Adding sugar to the racked young cider

This is an optional stage, though recommended if the juice wasn't sweetened earlier. Adding white sugar at this point will increase the alcoholic strength of the final cider and is especially useful if you started off with a juice that was low in natural sweetness.

Add granulated white sugar at the rate of 170g (about 6oz) to each gallon of young cider. Do this by first adding the sugar to a pan with the minimum of water needed when gently warmed to produce a syrup. This quantity of sugar will increase the gravity of the cider by 15 degrees and increase the alcoholic strength by about 2.5% by volume. There is no attempt here to try to produce a cider up to the maximum alcohol tolerance of the yeast – the intention is to produce ciders of moderate strength and excellent quality. You may, however, wish to experiment in producing ciders of greater alcoholic strength. Certainly, you could easily double or triple the above amount of sugar per gallon but if you do, remember that you will need to know that this is within the alcohol tolerance of the yeast, and be aware that the fermentation will take very much longer (with the cider certainly not being ready for

Christmas), and that beyond a certain point what you will be really making is more of an apple wine.

Having added the cooled sugar syrup, now top up the fermentation vessel with cold water to 2cm below the level of the bung with its fermentation lock and return the vessel preferably to its place at 60°F or 15°F, or in a warmer place if available and you wish to consume the cider sooner rather than later. Over the next day or two after adding the sugar syrup, the fermentation will again revive, though not as vigorously as before, and with time a smaller deposit of yeast will begin to settle to the bottom.

Left to continue to ferment, the cider will once again proceed to a natural dryness. The approach in this book is to do just this. If a dry cider is required, this fermented-out cider is simply bottled or stored in other suitable containers. If a medium dry, medium sweet, or sweet cider is desired, the approach is to ferment to dryness as above, then add further small quantities of white sugar syrup up to the desired taste, taking care to observe the procedures for storage (see below). This is an approach also used by some commercial manufacturers.

Making different still ciders

Dry still cider

To make this cider we need to use the racked, completely fermented-out young cider (whether having been through the sweetened stage or not). The appearance should be a hazy golden colour, its taste very dry, slightly acidic. Bubbles through the fermentation lock should have ceased or all but ceased. The hydrometer reading should be 1005 or below.

If the cider is unpalatably acidic at this stage, leave it in the demijohn or fermentation vessel for a month but move it to a warmer place where a slightly different kind of fermentation can occur, called the malolactic fermentation (brought about by a family of bacteria called *lactobacilli* – see Appendix 3) in which the more acidic malic acid is converted into the less acidic lactic acid. Taste at regular intervals until it seems, though still unmellow, rounder and more palatable. Whether going through this malolactic fermentation stage or not (if the cider is

Pick your day in October or November – you will be blessed with fine weather because cidermaking is a virtuous thing!

already palatably dry) now transfer to as *cold a place as possible* under lock. If fermenting at barrel volumes (9 gallons, 36 gallons etc.) rack one further time then leave the cider in the barrel in as cold a place as possible. When judged to be ready by taste, introduce the tap to the barrel and serve from this. Remember, however, that the cider will be in contact with a certain amount of yeast and, furthermore, how successfully the drink keeps in the barrel will depend on how quickly it is consumed (see Chapter 11). If operating at demi-john or 5–7 gallon plastic fermenter level, over the next few weeks, the cider will clear or remain slightly hazy without ever clearing completely: this is perfectly normal for some ciders, does not affect the drinking quality, and indeed is approved of in some quarters. There should have been no sign of activity in the cider or through the fermentation lock during this period. Rack off one last time from the small amount of yeast deposit that has formed at the bottom. Finally, add 2 Campden tablets and store the cider in any suitable containers, making certain they are filled well up to exclude air and that the tops are on securely. Storing in bottles is a very convenient means with screw or clip tops, or in corked wine bottles with a suitably designed label. Store in a cool, dark place where it will mature over the coming months, but is ready to start drinking as soon you regard it pleasant enough to do so.

Medium dry still cider

Instead of bottling the final racked clear(ish) cider above, we can now sweeten it a little with cooled white sugar syrup until it is to our taste or has an SG of about 1010. If the cider is very clear at this stage (that is, it is free or virtually free of yeast) it is safe to bottle this with a cork, *providing it is placed in a cold outhouse, shed or garage* (and, as an added precaution, 2 Campden tablets could be added here to kill any yeast that might have been brought through). The final product when opened may be very slightly spritzy, but will otherwise be still. If the cider is in any way cloudy or even significantly hazy, it is probably best stored in clean demi-johns under a fermentation lock, or vessels that have a pressure relief device, drinking it when you consider it pleasant to do so. Alternatively, the slight sweetening process of the dry cider can be undertaken just prior to drinking it.

Medium sweet and sweet still ciders

The same procedure is adopted for both of these, adding sugar syrup to about SG 1014–1018. Once again, for safety it is best to store these in demi-johns with a lock, or vessels with a pressure relief device, and place in a cold outhouse, shed or garage. Alternatively, the sweetening process can be done on the dry cider just prior to drinking. A further alternative is the use of artificial sweeteners such as saccharin, aspartame, sorbitol or lactose, this last being the most 'natural' of the options. All of these are non-fermentable substances and therefore allow these sweetened ciders to be bottled if so desired.

Making naturally conditioned bottled ciders

A naturally conditioned cider is one where the carbon dioxide is produced by a small secondary fermentation occurring in the bottle. Such ciders characteristically have a fizz and sparkle and are quite delicious. So-called 'champagne ciders' are perhaps the pinnacle of this type of sparkling cider, being of the very highest quality and traditionally bottled with the typical wiring to the cork.

Champagne cider

By a special technique known as *remuage* the yeast, which has been responsible for the conditioning, is also removed before wiring up the 'champagne' bottle. Remuage or 'riddling' involves keeping the bottle inverted and twisting it daily for about a week so that the yeast is worked down onto the cork. The neck of the bottle is then plunged into an ice/salt mixture to freeze the plug of yeast which can be ejected once the bottle is removed from the freezing mixture. The bottle is finally topped up with cider or water, before recorking and rewiring. Once again, this is not an especially difficult procedure, and you may wish to spend a little time trying it out, once you have made your sparkling ciders as described below.

Normally, a 'live' cider means having a very tiny layer of live yeast in the bottle and it is this type that is being considered here. The procedures indicated in this chapter produce very high quality conditioned ciders – dry, medium sweet, or sweet. Sparkling, naturally conditioned cider is best drunk well chilled, in smaller quantities, a bit like a fine white wine.

There are several important factors determining how quickly a bottled cider will acquire condition. These are:

- The amount of yeast in the bottle.
- The surrounding temperature.
- The length of time the cider is in the bottle.
- Sweetness (concentration of sugar).
- Type of bottle used.

If you want a delicious, naturally conditioned bottled cider, but one that avoids the possibility of burst bottles due to excessive build-up of carbon dioxide, *it is very important to observe the following*:

(1) Always make certain that the yeast in the bottle is an absolute minimum – *no more than the merest paint layer*. This will be achieved by making certain that the cider you are working with is racked to a haziness (only tiny amounts of suspended yeast deliberately brought through on racking) and not cloudy before bottling.

(2) Always keep the bottled cider in a cold outhouse, shed or garage.

(3) Assuming **1** and **2** are in place, the amount of condition will build up with time. It can take a couple of months with so little yeast and a cold environment before a nice sparkle develops. If you want to be certain of a degree of condition before this period of time, then keep the bottles in a warm (but not too warm!) environment for a week before putting them in the shed. You can also increase the amount of condition a short while prior to drinking by bringing the bottle into the warm, say for a few days, then refrigerate immediately before drinking. This stratagem should only be necessary if the cider hasn't long been in the bottle but for various reasons you want to drink it with a sparkle.

(4) Over time the concentration of sweetness in the bottle will govern the amount of condition. Assuming the alcoholic strength of the cider is well below the alcohol tolerance of the yeast, the tiny amount of yeast in the bottle will continue to ferment the sweetness of the dissolved sugar, building up the condition

continuously. This means that a bottle opened up, let us say, after six months will be extremely 'lively' and also with little if any remaining sweetness, since most/all of the residual sugar will have been fermented. The same bottle opened up after, say two months, will be moderately sparkling, and still sweetish.

(5) It is crucial that the bottles into which the cider is put are of the type that can take pressure. These include the old brown quart bottles with ceramic (later plastic) screw top and rubber seal; the 'clip top' type of beer bottles of various capacities; 'crown corked' beer bottles (plastic 'crowns' are also available which blow off if the pressure gets too great); commercial carbonated cider and soft drink bottles usually with a metal screw cap. There are others. It is now possible to buy or collect champagne-type glass bottles and to purchase either cork or plastic tops with the wiring for these bottles. Some people have also had success, for example, with the humble plastic carbonated soft drink bottles, and these may also be worth exploring, though be careful not to commit your whole batch to these in case of failure.

Always leave a space of 2.5cm (1in.) above the cider when bottling for naturally conditioned ciders. Bottles, however, which are quite *unsuitable* for conditioned ciders are wine bottles (pity, really, because there is an awful lot of these), squash drink bottles or indeed any bottle that originally was not designed to take pressure.

There are other methods of temporarily storing and serving these ciders which are discussed in Chapter 11.

Now for making these conditioned ciders!

Dry naturally conditioned cider

To make this cider we need to take the racked completely fermented out young cider (whether having been through the sweetening stage on page 59 or not), but such that this time a *little yeast sediment is brought through* so that we are working with a cider that is slightly hazy (not cloudy). To get to this stage may have involved a second racking stage (see the illustrated fermentation sheet on page 24). Now add white sugar syrup to the vessel equivalent to 1 level teaspoon of white sugar per pint or just less than 2 level teaspoons per litre. If you are using 1 gallon demi-johns, then add the sugar syrup, fit a rubber bung and while holding this, invert and shake the vessel to get the sugar completely evenly dissolved for a minute or so. If you are working with much larger volumes, add sugar syrup on a pro-rata basis and shake the vessel thoroughly to get the sugar evenly distributed. Now bottle, making certain that you leave a 2–3cm space between the top of the cider and the top or cap. Store in a cold, dark place, and referring again to the points regarding the build-up of condition in the cider, this sparkling dry cider should be ready to drink within 3 months or earlier (see the methods above for increasing the speed of conditioning).

Medium sweet naturally conditioned cider

Observe the above but this time add cooled sugar syrup in small quantities to the demi-john, shaking thoroughly each time, before tasting until the cider is *just sweet* to the taste – about SG 1014. It is very easy to oversweeten by mistake. Remember that carbon dioxide is itself acidic and that the conditioned cider you get to drink will actually be less sweet and more acidic than at this stage. Exactly how much less sweet and more acidic will, of course, depend on how long the bottle is stored before you drink it. If you are working with much larger volume vessels, say 5–6 gallon capacities, you will need to determine the amount of sugar syrup that is to your taste for 1 gallon by first syphoning off this volume into a specimen demi-john, and then adding the requisite amount of sugar syrup to the remaining bulk of cider on a pro-rata basis. Make certain, having done this, to spend a few minutes shaking the vessel (or even leave overnight) to ensure the sugar is evenly dissolved throughout the whole cider. Then bottle as above and store. Given the higher concentration of sugar in this cider, the conditioning will be ready earlier than for a dry cider, but is still likely to take at least a couple of months before there is anything appreciably formed by way of a sparkle.

Sweet naturally conditioned cider

Observe the above procedure but add sugar syrup in stages, shaking each time and tasting, until the cider is sweetish – be careful not to make it sickly. Having once added too much sugar, you cannot reverse it except possibly by blending it with a dry cider. As a guideline the SG should be of the order of 1018. Bottle and store as before. Once again, the conditioning will begin to develop appreciably after a couple of months.

Natural conditioning in bottles is an excellent way of producing this type of cider, and is perfectly safe, providing the above precautions are observed. It is inadvisable, however, to leave a naturally conditioned cider in a bottle much beyond 6 to 9 months, unless the bottles are thick-walled and very strong, of the champagne-type, for example. Other options for sweetening (as already discussed for still ciders) involves the addition of such sweeteners as saccharin, aspartame, sorbitol and lactose. If using these non-fermentable sweeteners, however, you will still need to add sugar at the rate of 1 level teaspoon per pint of cider to the bottle if you want the yeast to provide a natural condition to the cider.

Artificial conditioning

Most commercially produced sparkling cider is artificially conditioned by pumping in a small quantity of carbon dioxide under pressure then sealing the bottles. Nowadays relatively inexpensive devices are available for the small-scale cidermaker to do the same thing, if so desired, though there can be little doubt that a naturally conditioned bottled cider is a superior product.

However, there are advantages to artificial conditioning, namely that by putting the cider into the bottle 'bright' i.e. completely clear and then artificially carbonating before sealing the bottle, the possibility of excess carbon dioxide causing burst bottles is very largely removed. Effectively, the shelf life of such products is also much longer. In addition, the drinker doesn't have to wait for the conditioning to take place, although s/he will really have needed to successively cold racked to ensure that the cider is completely clear (free of yeast) before carbonating. Alternatively, the drink will have to be stabilised by pasteurisation or sulphiting (see Appendix 5) or be drunk within a short period of time.

Making medium dry, medium sweet and sweet ciders using traditional techniques **without adding sugar**

Remember that any fermentation left to continue to completion will always yield up a completely dry cider. If adopting a somewhat purist line where medium dry, medium sweet or sweet(ish) ciders are wanted but where there is no wish to add white sugar at all, or any other sweetener, then there are two important techniques available to the cidermaker. These are known as 'cold racking' and 'keeving'. Make sure that your mix of apples contains a higher proportion of dessert apples than otherwise: aim for an SG in the region of 1055.

Cold racking

This procedure for arriving at a cider of the desired sweetness involves tasting the developing young cider when the fermentation begins to slow down somewhat and/or using the hydrometer. Seek at the level of the preferred sweetness to influence the rate and course of the fermentation by placing the developing cider in as cold a situation as possible, then by successive rackings until fermentation ceases altogether. Replace lost volume due to removal of yeast/lees each time with cold water up to the neck of the fermentation vessel. Effectively, the fermentation will have been brought to a premature end by using as low a temperature as possible, and progressively shutting off the fermentation by removal of yeast as quickly as possible with successive rackings. Adding 1–2 Campden tablets per gallon or proprietary 'arresting' compounds can also be used to stop the fermentation. The SG for a medium dry cider would be about 1012, for a medium sweet cider about 1014 and for a sweet cider about 1018–1020. This is not a difficult procedure, but it is quite time consuming, and since you will have only fermented out a part of the natural sugars, your ultimate cider will be very weak in alcohol, unless the apples you started off with were very rich in sugar. On the other hand, it is often said that these ciders are fruitier than their sugar-sweetened counterparts.

Keeving

Keeving is an altogether more complicated process than 'cold racking' but is likely to be of interest especially to those cidermakers who are fascinated to try out these traditional techniques. The term itself probably arises from a 'keeve' or 'cuve' or from 'cuvage', all words from the French associated with vats, casks and fermentation. The idea which keeving exploits is to deliberately create a juice low in nutrient levels. In this way the fermentation throughout remains slow, and, coupled with periodic rackings, enables ciders to be produced that have never completely fermented out. There are similarities here of course with 'cold racking' but keeved ciders are characteristically brilliantly clear, lower in tannin than conventionally produced counterparts and usually quite delicious.

At the outset it is best to attempt the process during a cold period in order to discourage any premature fermentation and to reduce the risks of bacterial spoilage. The mix of fruit should bear a balance in favour of sweets or dessert apples (otherwise the juice will be short on sweetness) and ideally have come from old, unmanured/neglected orchards where the amount of soluble nitrogen and phosphorus is already low in the fruit.

The pulp is made in the normal manner, but instead of being pressed immediately is packed (not too tightly) into open-topped plastic barrels or dustbins and left to stand for a day when the process of steeping or 'maceration' (sometimes referred to as cuvage) encourages the leaching out of the pectin and the oxidation of tannin to produce a dark brown juice which is pressed out after the day's standing.

Over the coming week, left to its own devices this juice will ideally separate into a dark brown 'mucky' head, known by the French term as *chapeau brun* – on the bottom of the vessel a brown sediment of lees, and in between, a clear golden juice which can be syphoned off. The process actually occurs because natural enzymes in the apple juice convert pectin to pectic acid. Some of this combines with natural calcium in the juice to form a gel which rises along with tannin-oxidised apple

Syphoning off the clear juice after keeving

suspensions to form the brown *chapeau brun*, while some of the pectic acid combines with tannin to form a heavier product which sinks. To encourage this process add food grade calcium chloride at the rate of 2g per gallon to the initial pressed juice (traditionally, chalk and salt were used). Keep the juice cold. If you are successful with the keeving, you will be able to syphon off the very low nutrient juice in between the upper and lower solids. To witness this separating out of the juice can be remarkable and it usually occurs quite suddenly eg over the space of a few hours.

Now top up the juice with water if necessary, fit an airlock and *adding no yeast*, i.e. relying only on the natural *Saccharomyces* varieties present, wait for the fermentation to get underway. This will be very slow, but should be perceptible, throughout the winter and into spring. As usual make sure that for this process the ambient temperature is low but able to sustain the slow fermentation. The important thing is that you maintain control over the process so that you are in a position to rack off a more or less stable cider at whatever SG/sweetness you want. This should be of the order of 1018–1020 for a sweet cider and something like 1014 for a medium sweet.

If you want completely still ciders, and have no objection to sulphiting, add 2 Campden tablets per gallon of cider, bottle without a head space or store in bulk for consumption. If you do object to sulphiting, you will need to make certain the cider you finally bottle or store is perfectly clear and stable by racking and keeping cold. Alternatively, you can pasteurise if you have no objection (see Appendix 5). On the other hand, if you want naturally conditioned keeved ciders, don't sulphite but do bottle with the cider slightly hazy. Leave the usual 2.5cm gap at the head. Condition will develop over the coming months.

If the keeving process has *not* been successful, you will recognise this by the appearance after a few days of a creamy head on your pressed juice (instead of the dark brown 'debris'), indicative of a normal fermentation having got underway: the juice will not clear as it should for keeving, but will grow progressively turbid as the yeast population rapidly grows. If this happens, you will simply have to let it take its course and you will end up with a conventional – though doubtless still delicious – dry cider. You can, of course, sweeten this by whatever means if you so wish.

One final point is worth making here. Because the juice is being left

Plenty to talk about across the apple-bashing!

for as long as a week to keeve, the risk of serious infection from spoiling bacteria is a real one. It is advisable to sulphite the juice at the rate of 1 Campden tablet per gallon of expressed juice once this has been obtained and before the keeving process is underway. Do not sulphite later as this will destroy the low concentrations of *Saccharomyces* species which you need.

To summarise, you may wish to attempt this traditional technique but perhaps in the first instance it would be worth experimenting with a small volume of juice to see how you get on. There can be little doubt that some of the finest ciders are produced by slow fermentation of nutrient-deficient juices, but it is also true that you will need a degree of luck.

There are certainly many dedicated small-scale cidermakers who operate this way, and these two techniques have long been traditional in making cider in France (indeed, the keeving process is sometimes referred to as the making of French cider) where regulations prohibit the addition of any artificial sweetening, including sugar. In Britain, however, there never were any such regulations and, once sugar became a cheaper commodity in the nineteenth century, the preference for sugar sweetening of a dry cider and then inducing a slow secondary fermentation in the barrel was a much preferred technique for its reliability. The result was a naturally conditioned sparkling cider with its own protective 'head' of carbon dioxide, but would still require a care and dedication on the part of the cellarman.

At the commercial level, manufacturers of cider don't go to the trouble of keeving or successive racking. They usually ferment out to dryness, then sweeten with non-fermentable saccharine or sorbitol, or pasteurise and sweeten with sugar. Alternatively, they may 'sterilise'

by 0.45 micron filtration of the yeast and suspensions and then do the above. They may reintroduce a small amount of yeast if they want a 'live' cider, or pasteurise and then artificially carbonate or leave the cider still. Most of this technology nowadays is actually available to the small-scale cidermaker, but you have to decide whether you want to go down that road. Pasteurisation is

considered in Appendix 5 and is undoubtedly a powerful means of stabilising a cider with minimum fuss, allowing, for example, the retailer to be certain that none of his/her bottled product will ever be subject to bursts. However, for most cidermakers at the small-scale level, much of the technology is not necessary and some deplore it. By an understanding of the processes involved and using the skills outlined above we can make whatever ciders we want without recourse to such things as plate filters, pasteurisation, artificial sweeteners or artificial conditioning.

Fermentation in 8 easy steps

1   Put vessel containing juice in a warm place if possible (kitchen ideal) and add 2 level teaspoons of yeast with nutrients per gallon of juice. Plug opening loosely with clean cotton wool.

2   When fermentation quietens (after 2–3 days) clean neck of vessel and fit fermentation lock.

3   Ferment to dryness (6 weeks to 3 months depending on temperature and apple varieties) or until cider has largely cleared and bubbles ceased, SG 1005 or less. The following stages 4 and 5 are optional.

4   Rack off. Add 170 g (6 oz) of white sugar as a syrup to each gallon of racked young cider and return to warm place if possible.

5   Ferment to dryness as for Stage 3 above.

6   Rack off and move to as cold a place as possible for 2–3 weeks until cider clears or very nearly so.

7   To make still ciders, now rack again.

a   For dry still cider: If cider is clear, simple bottle or barrel, leave to mature before drinking. If not clear, stabilise by either adding two Campden tablets per gallon of cider, or pasteurise or filter.

b   For a medium sweet still cider: Add white sugar syrup carefully to SG 1012–1015 and store cider in demi-john or barrel under lock until required and ready for drinking. Alternatively, store dry and sweeten just prior to consumption. If wishing to bottle, only do so after having stabilised cider by adding two Campden tablets per gallon or better, pasteurising or sterile filtering.

8   To make conditioned ciders, first rack again as for Stage 7, but bring through a little yeast.

a   For dry conditioned cider: Add 4 level teaspoons of white sugar per gallon of cider. Bottle in vessels that can take pressure. Store in cool dark place for 2–3 months to allow condition to develop. Do not sulphite or pasteurise.

b   For medium sweet/sweet conditioned cider: Add white sugar as a cooled syrup to SG 1012–1018 and bottle in vessels that can take pressure. Store in a cool dark place for 2–3 months to allow condition to develop. Do not sulphite or pasteurise.

sparkling **CIDER**

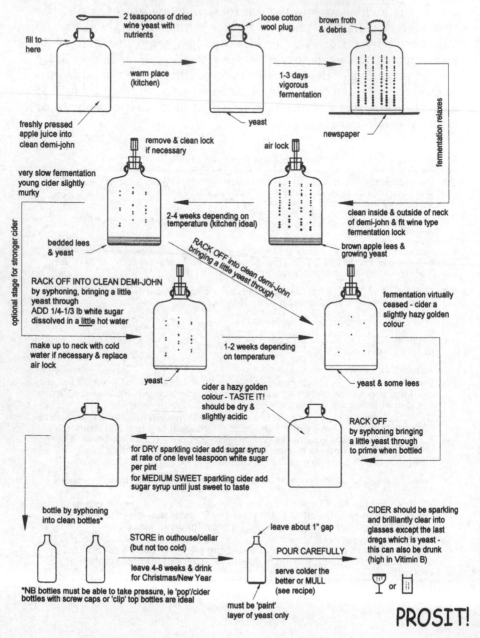

fill to → here

2 teaspoons of dried wine yeast with nutrients

warm place (kitchen)

freshly pressed apple juice into clean demi-john

yeast

loose cotton wool plug

1-3 days vigorous fermentation

brown froth & debris

newspaper

fermentation relaxes

remove & clean lock if necessary

air lock

very slow fermentation young cider slightly murky

2-4 weeks depending on temperature (kitchen ideal)

clean inside & outside of neck of demi-john & fit wine type fermentation lock

bedded lees & yeast

brown apple lees & growing yeast

RACK OFF into clean demi-john bringing a little yeast through

optional stage for stronger cider

RACK OFF INTO CLEAN DEMI-JOHN by syphoning, bringing a little yeast through ADD 1/4-1/3 lb white sugar dissolved in a <u>little</u> hot water

make up to neck with cold water if necessary & replace air lock

yeast

1-2 weeks depending on temperature

fermentation virtually ceased - cider a slightly hazy golden colour

yeast & some lees

cider a hazy golden colour - TASTE IT! should be dry & slightly acidic

for DRY sparkling cider add sugar syrup at rate of one level teaspoon white sugar per pint
for MEDIUM SWEET sparkling cider add sugar syrup until just sweet to taste

RACK OFF by syphoning bringing a little yeast through to prime when bottled

bottle by syphoning into clean bottles*

STORE in outhouse/cellar (but not too cold)

leave 4-8 weeks & drink for Christmas/New Year

*NB bottles must be able to take pressure, ie 'pop'/cider bottles with screw caps or 'clip' top bottles are ideal

leave about 1" gap

POUR CAREFULLY

serve colder the better or MULL (see recipe)

must be 'paint' layer of yeast only

CIDER should be sparkling and brilliantly clear into glasses except the last dregs which is yeast - this can also be drunk (high in Vitimin B)

or

PROSIT!

still CIDER

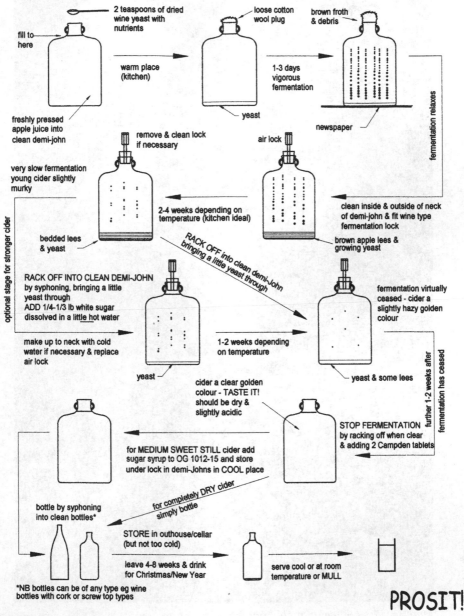

2 teaspoons of dried wine yeast with nutrients

loose cotton wool plug

brown froth & debris

fill to here

warm place (kitchen)

1-3 days vigorous fermentation

fermentation relaxes

freshly pressed apple juice into clean demi-john

yeast

newspaper

remove & clean lock if necessary

air lock

very slow fermentation young cider slightly murky

2-4 weeks depending on temperature (kitchen ideal)

clean inside & outside of neck of demi-john & fit wine type fermentation lock

bedded lees & yeast

brown apple lees & growing yeast

optional stage for stronger cider

RACK OFF into clean demi-john bringing a little yeast through

RACK OFF INTO CLEAN DEMI-JOHN by syphoning, bringing a little yeast through ADD 1/4-1/3 lb white sugar dissolved in a little hot water

fermentation virtually ceased - cider a slightly hazy golden colour

make up to neck with cold water if necessary & replace air lock

1-2 weeks depending on temperature

yeast

yeast & some lees

further 1-2 weeks after fermentation has ceased

cider a clear golden colour - TASTE IT! should be dry & slightly acidic

STOP FERMENTATION by racking off when clear & adding 2 Campden tablets

for MEDIUM SWEET STILL cider add sugar syrup to OG 1012-15 and store under lock in demi-johns in COOL place

for completely DRY cider simply bottle

bottle by syphoning into clean bottles*

STORE in outhouse/cellar (but not too cold)

leave 4-8 weeks & drink for Christmas/New Year

serve cool or at room temperature or MULL

*NB bottles can be of any type eg wine bottles with cork or screw top types

PROSIT!

More scratting of the quartered apples prior to pressing.

11 Blending, Storing and Serving the Cider

Some of the old scrumpy was so sharp and strong, you might need two men to hold you down to drink it! I've heard it described as strong enough to burn the name off a tombstone, but it is probably nearer the truth to say that most farm cider was quite weak. Given the arduous labour of haymaking and harvest, cider quenched the thirst and replaced lost fluid, and more often than not was healthier than any water available.

Blending is a most enjoyable art since it involves a great deal of tasting, judging and discussion – with oneself if necessary, but much better fun if done in company.

Most retailed ciders – even those from small-scale cidermakers – are blended products. This is because apart from a very limited number of vintage cider apple cultivars, such as Kingston Black or Stoke Red, most 'single varietal' ciders are lacking in one respect or another, and need to be blended with others to produce a cider of character.

If you have followed the techniques developed throughout this book, especially those concerned with establishing a 'balanced' juice through mixing the fruit at the outset and/or corrections to tannin, acid and sugar levels of the juice, there should be little need for blending.

However, if you have access to a range of different cider cultivars, there are advantages to pressing and fermenting single variety juices and then blending the final ciders to the product you want. Seasoned cidermakers who operate this way clearly want the control over the processes (especially if retailing the product) which blending ciders has over the more 'organic', less systematic means of blending the fruit itself. Besides, it is probably the only way of really getting to know the characteristics of each of the cider apple cultivars and their resultant ciders. This can be especially important as the basis of that really creative dimension to cidermaking in enabling ciders with 'customised' characteristics to be made.

Blending, then, is used to produce a superior cider out of individuals (either single varietals or otherwise) which are considered to be imbalanced or capable of improvement. The process can also be used to remedy poor ciders but should never be thought capable of rectifying a cider smitten with problems. Gross defects sometimes occur and you should discard such ciders without sorrow, treating their loss and your estimation of the reasons for the problems as all part of the developing experience in the craft. (Having said that, some apparently irredeemable ciders if left for a very long time in bottle or bulk storage have been known to miraculously resurrect themselves!)

If you are intending blending, you can do so for almost all characteristics: body, insipidity, sweetness/dryness, acidity, colour etc. The underlying principle behind blending involves bringing together ciders that are compatible but with opposite characteristics.

Remember, if blending to follow these rules:

- Always trial your blending on a small scale first, using measured proportions, before treating the bulk.
- Always make sure that ciders you intend blending have been racked and are stable i.e. prior to final storage before drinking. If possible always blend ciders of a similar age.
- Recognise that because of differences in the levels of sweetness (residual or otherwise), nutrients, acidity and any yeast present that blending can result in a short period of re-fermentation, so that you should expect to have to delay for a few days the final bulk storage or bottling until the new blended cider has re-stabilised.
- Blending may result in the appearance of hazes, sometimes after delays of various lengths.

■ It is better, if possible, to blend an overdry cider with a sweet one (and vice versa) rather than by the use of sugar.

Storing and dispensing the cider

While it is true that most ciders will mature for several weeks, or even months, as their flavours stabilise and smooth out, in general the drink does not profit by any extended ageing.

There are many methods of storing, dispensing and serving the cider. Some of the options have already been touched upon and they are further discussed here. It is really a question of what volumes of the drink are being consumed over what period of time. Most retailed still cider of the types being discussed, made by traditional craftsmen, recommend being consumed within a short period of time – a bottle on the day of opening, for example. This is because once exposed to the air, cider is apt to quickly sharpen and sour. The higher-alcohol ciders have a slightly greater protection, but still far short of a wine which even at 11–13% alcohol will quickly sour. This problem of storage and dispensing cider dogs the retail industry, since unless a retailer has a guaranteed volume of sales s/he is reluctant even to take on a polypin of cider. If it cannot be drunk quickly, it will sour in the vessel, become unpalatable, discourage both the potential convert drinker and retailer, and have to be thrown away. The net effect is to depress the interest in cider.

The situation covering the oxidation of cider was ever thus, but at least in traditional cidermaking and drinking areas there was/is a much greater demand for the product, and an oak barrel of cider, providing it is kept in a very cool back bar or cellar or other appropriate place, can still serve up a pleasant glass, months after the barrel has been broached. True, there is also the small matter of an older generation's liking or acceptance of a harsher, scrumpy-type cider. Nowadays, both drinker and retailer are looking for a consistently fresh product, though one which is still a real cider, available and served proudly from 'up front'.

These problems need not affect the small-scale maker and drinker of cider to anywhere near the same degree. Corked bottled dry cider probably has a good shelf life of a year and is a convenient small volume means of consumption. Transferring dry, medium sweet or sweet cider from a demi-john into a jug for the social occasion is as good a way of dispensing as any, though the balance of the demi-john even under a lock will have to be consumed within a relatively short period of time: weeks at most. Clearly, much larger volumes such as in a polypin can be consumed quickly if serving the needs of a party.

There is, however, another means of dispensing these still ciders from bulk where it is possible to draw off a glass at a time and still keep the cider fresh over a period of time. This is the 'manucube', which involves an outer rigid box, and an inner collapsible bag. As the cider is drawn off by means of a tap the bag collapses and air cannot enter to spoil the cider. This type which has become common at a 3-litre level for wine, the so-called 'wine box', can be used for the amateur's cider. Such boxes can be saved, opened up, the tap mechanism removed, the collapsible bag rinsed out and then filled with cider. It has a shelf life of some weeks, as for wine. Alternatively, manucubes are available commercially relatively cheaply.

The manucube is not suitable for dispensing conditioned cider because of the presence of the carbon dioxide. Serve naturally conditioned cider chilled and straight from the bottle, or even very cold as for a good white wine, into wine glasses or tumblers, exercising care not to disturb the tiny amount of yeast sediment, which can be drunk separately. This type of cider is usually very clear if it has been left long enough in a cold environment.

12 Troubleshooting

"Oh, I've not made cider since 1939, the year they brought in rationing. We had an evacuee, a young girl, from London staying with us in the country in Oxfordshire at the time. One evening, we were waiting for dinner round the table in the kitchen when there was the most almighty explosion. Our heads went down instinctively, thinking a doodlebug must have hit us! After a minute we peered up, trying to figure out the surrounding mayhem. And what had happened? A bottle of 'Ciderex' had exploded from the warmth of the range, shot upwards, hit the underside of the shelf on which was set all the family crockery and sent the lot showering into pieces over the kitchen floor! I'm not sure a doodlebug wouldn't have made less mess!"

Despite good working practices (not that keeping 'live' cider by a range is!), inevitably things will go wrong from time to time. This chapter is devoted to signs, symptoms, diagnoses and suggested remedies. It is worth saying, however, that by following the procedures and acquiring the skills established in the earlier parts of this book, your need of this chapter will be very rare.

Slimy apple pulp

Genuine cider fruit rarely causes this problem, but mixed apple pulp having a high proportion of dessert fruit can turn out to be unmanageably slimy, clogging up the press-cloths of the cheese and reducing yield considerably. The problem doesn't really affect the use of a simple basket press because the volumes of pulp being used are much smaller and the arrangement is much simpler.

Cutting out all rot will minimise patulin and a host of other potential troubles.

Changing the mix of apples with more cider or culinary varieties will certainly help by restoring the 'structure' of the pulp, which ideally should be granular. There are also proprietary 'mixers' available such as rice husks (which mimic the action of the old straw in improving the drainage channels for the juice and minimising clogging). Perhaps the best solution is to thoroughly mix in 2 tablespoons per 'gallon' of pulp of pectolytic enzyme and leave to stand overnight. The idea here is for the released pectin which is responsible for the sliminess to be broken down by the enzyme. This usually works well and the resultant pulp will press well. Note that if you had intended adding pectolytic enzyme to the juice as a preventative against pectin haze the need for this will be obviated by any additions already made to solve the problem of sliminess.

Sluggish or failed fermentation

It is crucial that the fermentation gets underway as soon after pressing the apple juice as possible. Make certain that the dried wine yeast being used is fresh or well within the date stamp on the batch. If the yeast is old or smells 'off' it will fail to get going and can even sour the apple juice. Ensure that the wine yeast used is of a type that contains those nutrients needed by the yeast for its growth.

If you preferred to let the natural wild yeast do the fermenting and yet after three or four days there seems no sign of activity (vigorous frothing at the mouth of the vessel) then you have a problem. Unless you are prepared to accept the prospect of losing the juice (or possibly as a last resort drinking it), you may have to set aside your scruples and pitch with a proprietary dried yeast compound as above. A 'starter' bottle of yeast can always be made up prior to pitching, so that when you do so, you know the yeast is well and alive and working before going into the juice. To make a starter bottle add a couple of teaspoons of dried yeast with nutrients and a teaspoon of white sugar to a half pint beer bottle or similar. Now add 3–4 fl oz or, say, 100ml of tepid/warm water and swirl thoroughly. Plug loosely with sterile cotton wool and put in a warm place. Within a few hours, the yeast will be seen to have started working by the tiny bubbles issuing from the settled yeast causing a head or froth to appear. Swirl round thoroughly and pitch into the juice, giving this a good rousing with a sterilised wooden stick or spoon to aerate the juice thoroughly since *Saccharomyces* yeasts need oxygen in the initial stages of their fermentation. Thereafter, they function anaerobically. By such measures with luck you may save the batch. The other major reason for a sluggish or failed fermentation is quite simply that the ambient temperature is too cold. If the fermentation is 'stuck', move the vessel into a distinctly warm place (such as a warm place in a kitchen). Once again, with luck the fermentation will get underway. If not, apply remedies as above. After it has picked up, you can move the vessel back away from the warm source into a more convenient location providing the ambient temperature is at least about 54°F–60°F/12°C–15°C.

Acetification

Do not confuse this with a straightforward natural acidity in your final cider (due to malic acid) which, although making an unbalanced drink and unpalatable for some people, for many others is not actually unpleasant as such. The product is simply deemed a little harsh. Sweetening will ameliorate this acidity but sourness due to acetification is an altogether different matter.

There are a number of routes by which cider becomes acetified but in all of them air plays an important role in allowing the bacterium *Acetobacter* to flourish. It is this organism which is responsible, found in and requiring air for the oxidation of the alcohol in the cider to ethanoic acid (acetic acid). This in dilute solution is none other than vinegar and the cider takes on a most disagreeable vinegary taste. If attack has been slight before identification, it is possible to neutralise the acid with potassium carbonate, but once again prevention is much better than cure.

Unclean and unsterilised equipment is also a source of infection. However, one of the most important source of this acetifying bacteria must be the vinegar fly or fruit fly, *Drosophila melanogaster* which harbours the bacteria in large numbers and which, if allowed onto the apple juice or the developing cider at any time, will do its worst. Beware of it – it appears magically around any opened fermenting vessel or body of fruit juice! This is why it is important at every stage of cidermaking that the juice is covered or under airlock, the only exceptions to this being the necessary procedures for actually making the cider such as racking, taking hydrometer readings or bottling, all of which should be performed as efficiently as possible in terms of time and with as little aeration as possible. Remember, the juice at the outset of the process is actually at its most vulnerable to infection because it has not yet acquired through the fermentation process a protective 'head' of carbon dioxide.

Thus, to minimise the chances of acetification it is important to ensure that the juice is lightly plugged with new clean cotton wool until fermentation gets going, that the neck of the vessels are cleaned and fermentation locks fitted as soon as necessary, that the fermentation proceeds steadily, that the young cider is then stored in such a manner (in demi-johns, casks, barrels, under lock, or bottles topped up to the cork for dry ciders or with a 'safety gap' of 2.5cm for conditioned cider) that air is excluded. When racking, transferring from one vessel to another, removing samples for hydrometer readings etc., always at the end of the operation make up the loss of any juice by topping up with cold water to exclude air. Other reasons for souring due to acetification can be the use of yeast which is 'off', or in the case of bottling, by the use of inferior corks for dry ciders and having faulty seals in the case of conditioned ciders, both examples allowing air in with consequent spoilage. Similarly, bottles which have been sterilised with metabisulphite solution and not rinsed out with cold water can spell death to any yeast which may be put into the bottle, say, for natural conditioning: the resulting cider will not condition, the safety gap of air above will work on the cider to sour it.

At the end of the day, if the spoilage is just too great, you will either have to discard the product or, if you are lucky, use it in the kitchen for culinary purposes: cider vinegar is actually wonderful stuff in this capacity but not as a drink (certainly not in any quantity). A different sort of souring can also affect cider, some of which is also due to aerobic micro-organisms. The cider is clearly 'off', with a very poor smell, unpleasant, even acrid to taste. This is due to a whole complex of reactions, including infection from other airborne organisms, and bacterial decay of the dead yeast and apple lees. If any or all of this occurs, the resultant mess will simply have to be thrown away!

Film yeasts ('flowers')

These wild yeasts are mostly of the *Candida* family and occur on the fruit itself and in the air. They will quickly infect any juice that is moribund in its fermentation or any improperly stored cider, especially if the yeast has already got into the juice/cider and now finds itself in contact with air.

Wash fruit thoroughly in the preparatory stages to juice making. Older fruit and damaged windfalls will need to be looked over particularly carefully. Get the fermentation off to a flying start; keep air well off the juice or developing cider; avoid 'stuck' fermentations. Whatever means of storing cider you are using, keep the vessels well topped up to exclude air, but remember if making a naturally conditioned cider you must preserve a 2.5cm head space.

Some people advise, as a general prophylactic to this problem, sulphiting the juice before fermentation – sulphur dioxide is certainly extremely toxic to film yeasts – but use will depend on how you feel about sulphiting. Typical symptoms are those of a white powdery film on the surface of the cider with heavier infestations breaking up as greasy plates that sink to the bottom of the drink. There is often an attendant sourness and taste and smell of ethyl ethanoate (ethyl acetate) characteristic of 'pear drops' or nail varnish solvent. At higher concentrations most people find this very unpleasant. Infection at this level results in the cider sadly having to be thrown away and all of the equipment and storage vessels thoroughly sterilised before any re-use. If the problem is recognised very early on with little damage, then it is best to add 2 Campden tablets per gallon of juice/cider to prevent any further growth and then set up a trial blending with good cider. You may get away with it, but don't blend in volume before having satisfied yourself it really can be saved. If in doubt, dispose of it. Bottled or otherwise stored cider which is naturally conditioning with carbon dioxide at the head will not be attacked by *Candida* film yeasts.

Cider 'sickness'

Sweet ciders, low in acidity, occasionally suffer from this disorder. Low acid ciders are always more prone to infection, anyway. Typically, the cider acquires a faint milky haze and rather sweet aldehyde flavours with the drink becoming very unpalatable. The problem appears to be brought about during fermentation by a family of bacteria known as *Zymomonas* which are involved in the partial oxidation of the developing alcohol especially to the aldehyde ethanal (formerly acetaldehyde). Little can be done but to discard the afflicted drink, not least because the implicated organisms are entirely resistant to sulphur dioxide. Once again, if the problem is caught early enough, you can try fermenting the cider out to dryness by adding nutrients and a new wine yeast culture from a starter bottle, and subsequently attempting to blend the product with good cider in the hope of ending up with an acceptable drink. As with all blending operations, however, do run it first on a trial basis; if in doubt, discard it.

'Ropiness'

So-called 'ropiness' or 'oiliness' sometimes affects ciders and wines that have been long in store. The drink pours in a thick syrup-like fashion and although there is little alteration to the flavour, the texture is universally repellent. The condition seems to come about through a proliferation of lactic acid bacteria whose role in the malolactic fermentation has been considered and which is generally welcomed. However, here it is not. Vigorous stirring or/and fining/filtering to remedy or ameliorate the problem is sometimes cited, but unless this is entirely successful, the cider will need to be thrown away. Sulphiting at the rate of 2 Campden tablets per gallon prior to storage is usually successful as a preventative if the condition seems to afflict your cidermaking.

Mouse taint

A generally regarded offensive taint of mice due to the formation of ethanamide (formerly acetamide) can occur in some ciders. (Some people even claim it should be thought of as an integral part of the rich array of flavours in a real cider!) Fortunately, its appearance is unusual, though seemingly capricious. It is actually due to wild yeasts of the *Brettanomyces* family along with some *lactobacilli* which have infected the apple juice and operate a minor but damaging fermentation parallel to the principal *Saccharomyces* fermentation to alcohol. Thorough cleaning of the apples is important. The best prophylactic is 2 Campden tablets per gallon of juice (100ppm SO_2) which destroys this spoilage organism; remember, do not pitch with proprietary wine yeast until at least 24–36 hours have elapsed if sulphiting.

If the problem appears in the cider, suggested treatments vary. The most popular seems to be the use of activated charcoal at the rate of 1 tablespoon per gallon to absorb the offending chemical, followed by racking, filtering and blending. As with all these problems, reprieve for the cider usually depends on the extent to which the problem has taken hold. Frankly, for such a problem we would recommend discarding the cider, with the usual need for scrupulous cleaning and sterilisation of equipment before re-use.

Haziness

Properly made and properly managed, stored long enough under the right circumstances, almost all ciders will turn out clear – even brilliantly clear – without the need of filtration or finings. Having said that, some ciders are reluctant to clear. It is also worth noting that people have different attitudes towards haziness in their alcoholic drinks. Nowadays there is little tolerance, for example, to even slightly hazy beer, let alone cloudiness. They want the beer to be 'bright'. This is understandable since cloudiness in a beer usually involves some suspended yeast and this, even if not unpleasant to taste, can interfere with, rather than add to, the flavour of the drink itself. However, often the yeast does impart an unpleasant flavour which is obviously unacceptable.

In the case of cider the situation is both similar and different. Firstly, and most importantly, there has been a long tradition of drinking cider which quite naturally turned out somewhat cloudy or hazy. Indeed, in many quarters the cider would almost be viewed with suspicion if it were not cloudy – at least it would prove it was real cider! This is because often, depending on the mix of apples, and the circumstances of fermentation, the suspensions are either not yeast, or not largely yeast, but products of the apples themselves and therefore can be regarded as adding to the rich and complex flavours associated with real cider.

Principal amongst these 'natural' reasons for haziness in cider is that due to pectin in the apple (this has been described earlier). There is a good case to be made for adding pectolytic enzyme to the juice prior to fermentation, especially if the mix of apples contains a high proportion of long-stored apples or/and dessert varieties, since it is in these that the pectin is richest and the possibility of pectin haze the greatest. Adding the enzyme to a cider that has developed the problem, prior or during bulk storage, for example, may clear it but the haze is actually caused by unbroken down pectin being thrown out of solution by the developing alcohol, so the efficacy of the treatment at this stage is much less than addition at the juice stage. Tannin hazes or deposits sometimes arise from the use of tannin-rich fruit, such as a preponderance of bittersweet apples in the mix. Too high a concentration of tannin in solution can mean that upon cooling, such as refrigeration prior to drinking, the tannin is precipitated out of solution as a haze. This is particularly annoying if the cider has been bottled perfectly clear. Since tannin is a significant part of the character of a cider, the object must be to retain a balance of this, but it has to be said that under normal circumstances you would be very unlucky to find yourself so afflicted with this problem. Sometimes the haziness is due to suspended yeast, sometimes working its way into a colloidal state which may prove very difficult to clear. There is some evidence to suggest that pure strains of proprietary wine yeasts bed down better than reliance on wild yeasts to perform the fermentation.

Opalescence in the cider will almost always result from an unwelcome formation of ethyl ethanoate (ethyl acetate) producing the unpleasant smell/taste of 'pear drops' either by *Candida* yeasts (film yeasts as discussed earlier) or for chemical or other biochemical reasons (see below).

At the end of the day, however, most ciders will clear or almost clear naturally, especially if they are put in a cold enough environment. In the case of naturally conditioned (carbonated) bottled ciders, it is important that the cider is bottled in a *slightly* hazy state due to a small amount of suspended yeast being needed. Over the storage months, this beds down as a 'paint layer' on the bottom and, of course, produces a natural sparkle to the cider.

If you are concerned to produce ciders which are always perfectly or brilliantly clear (so-called 'polishing'), you may very well wish to experiment with the kind of range of proprietary finings available or any of the filtration devices.

Finings of whatever type (and there are many) exploit the fact that hazes are caused by materials with electrically charged particles of one polarity, while the choice of fining comprises electrically charged particles of an opposite polarity. The net effect is an electrical neutralisation reaction in which the haze material hopefully is thrown out of solution as a suspension and the resultant cider, after filtration, ends up beautifully clear!

Two of the most widely used finings are gelatine and bentonite. This latter is particularly versatile and well regarded in winemaking circles. It is a montmorillonite clay $(Al_2O_3.4SiO_2.H_2O)$, widely available, and is especially good for ridding ciders of protein hazes and cloudiness. It needs to be added as a suspension in water at a dosage recommended by the manufacturers, but can actually be added to the juice as a powder at the outset of fermentation and is reputed to lead to near miraculously clear ciders, leaving behind a well-compacted sediment, ready for racking off. As with all these things, it is best to perform trials, using a number of different fining preparations to establish efficacies and dosages particular to each problem.

There can be no doubt that clearing a stubbornly hazy/cloudy cider with one of these products can give you a real fillip – especially if you feel you have reprieved a product you thought lost – but in general there is a sneaking feeling that having to resort to filters and finings and so forth is, at the end of the day, something of a confession of failure.

Flat or unconditioned cider in the bottle

The above point concerning unrinsed out bottles having had sterilising fluid in them is relevant here. Faulty seals or chipped glass tops on the bottles is another source of lack of condition. Check these before bottling and discard any that are dubious. Similarly, bottling in an inappropriate bottle i.e. one that is not designed to take pressure, will not produce any condition.

A cider may appear to come out of its bottle without the expected fizz and sparkle for the simple reason that it hasn't been in

Ideal bottle types for naturally conditioned cider

the bottle long enough. As we noted in the section on natural conditioning, this process depends on a number of factors including the temperature, quantity of yeast, and length of time in the bottle. *Do not,* however, in order to speed up the conditioning, increase the quantity of yeast beyond a 'paint layer' or the ambient temperature beyond cool or cold. If you do, the following will result!

Burst bottles

These are due to any or all of the following: too much yeast, too warm a temperature, too high a concentration of sugar, too great a length of time in the bottle, too thin-walled a bottle, failure to leave a 2.5cm (1in.) gap at the top of cider. Follow the strictures in the section on natural conditioning and you will never have any problems. Always store in the dark in an outhouse or shed. Don't bottle up cider for conditioning unless you intend drinking it within a reasonable period of time. The worst thing you can do is to bottle up, and then leave it in a shed or garage and forget about it.

If you suspect that you may have too much yeast after it has bedded down, then it is better to open up and re-bottle. There will be no loss of quality. If you suspect the temperature, say in summer, to be too warm, then move the bottles to a colder place. Above all, cautiously test one or two bottles after a few weeks/months to gauge the amount of condition. If you get deluged in the fountain, then there is far too much condition and you should release the pressure carefully on all of the bottles! Drink up quickly thereafter, or repeat the pressure release operation.

Cider tasting of 'pear drops'

This is a rare but, when it occurs, usually terminal problem. The resulting cider is usually quite unpalatable and will need to be thrown away. The active ingredient in pear drop sweets is an ester called ethyl ethanoate (formerly called ethyl acetate). This is a naturally occurring product (not poisonous) of pears and a number of other fruits, including many varieties of apple, though in very low quantities, and in the fruit it has an undoubtedly pleasant taste. However, it can be produced in cider at unacceptable levels (often along with small amounts of other esters) and imparts a most unpleasant flavour to the drink.

It appears to come about by the reaction between the alcohol and ethanoic acid (acetic) from the partial oxidation product of some of the alcohol under the right conditions. These reactions may be partially microbiological in origin, as alluded to earlier in the case of *Candida* film yeasts. There are two principal situations which either separately or together will lead to this problem. If the cider is fermented at too high a temperature (for example, right up close to a radiator, or constantly near to an open fire, or some other excessive source of warmth) the possibility of the above pear drops ester being produced is considerably increased. Thus, it is permissible to ferment at higher temperatures up to 70°F/21°C (about warm room temperature e.g. a kichen) but beyond this the possibility of the above reaction increases considerably. The other reason, almost certainly compounded by higher temperatures, is when the fermentation goes on so long in contact with a large settled mass of apple lees. Some pressed juices are very thick and produce, as the fermentation get underway, a large settled mass of brown lees. If the juice is particularly sweet, the fermentation at this stage can continue for a long time in contact with these lees, increasing the risk of the undesirable ester. The answer is to rack off at a much earlier stage.

Thus, when the fermentation has slackened off, and the lees have distinctly settled down (they may be flocculent), rack off from these, top up with cold water and continue the fermentation to dryness. Now rack off again (that is, to the first racking stage as discussed in Chapter 10, *Fermentation*) and add the white sugar syrup to the young cider and proceed as normal. Effectively, you have introduced an earlier racking stage to remove the body of the fermenting cider from an excess of lees.

You may, on drinking a glass of real cider, detect a very slight sense of this pear drop ester. At this concentration it is quite likely to be pleasant and to add to the overall cocktail of flavours which comprise a real cider.

13 A Pipkin of Drinks, A Dish of Recipes

The drinks

Apart from the pleasure of drinking the cider in its own right, there are many drinks to be made from it. Given below are just a sample, all of them particularly delicious because the cider is home-made and fresh.

Winter's Delight Mulled Cider

A delicious drink for a cold winter's night. Make sure you've been out in the cold beforehand, or if preparing it for a party, that the guests have come as thoroughly chilled to the bone as possible!

Ingredients
For approximately 1 quart or 1 litre of fresh cider use:
12 whole cloves
1 good stick of cinnamon

12 white/green cardamom seeds
Pinch of grated nutmeg

Method

Choose a suitable mulling vessel – avoid aluminium or non-stick, but a glass or ordinary stainless steel pan is suitable. A stainless steel 'maslin pan' of 2–3 litre capacity is ideal.

Gently simmer the cider with the spices for 20 minutes or so. Dissolve a little white sugar into the mulled cider according to preferred taste and serve hot in a tumbler or wine glass.

For a drink with a slightly bigger 'kick', add a measure of light or dark rum to each glass beforehand.

Summer Cider Punch

For those glorious hot summer days, try this.
In a large bowl to each quart or litre of **really cold** cider add:
1 litre of cold lemonade or soda water
Cut up peeled rind of an unwaxed lemon
Juice of half a lemon
1 measure of whisky
1 measure of gin
A little caster sugar to sweeten to preferred taste

As variants upon this, replace the lemon peel with any or all of pieces of orange, cucumber, mint or other similar herbs.

Hot Cider Toddy

For colds or just as a nice drink.
In a stainless steel or enamelled pan simmer for a minute ¼ litre (about ½ pint) of cider with:
2 cloves
A little crudely chopped up root ginger
Twist of lemon juice
Strain off into a glass and add a dessertspoon of honey.

Recipes using cider

Cider has long been used in recipes associated with pork with which it goes beautifully. In fact, it is especially good with any light meat – chicken, rabbit and even fish.

Pork with Cider & Cream

Serves 4: preparation and cooking time 45 mins or less.

Ingredients

¼ litre or ½ pint dry cider
4 pork chops or steaks
1 medium sized onion
50g or 2oz mushrooms
2 tablespoons plain flour
Salt and pepper
60g or 2oz butter
150 ml or ¼ pint single cream
1 tablespoon chopped parsley
1 tablespoon chopped chives

Method

Chop the onion finely. In a deep frying pan, melt the butter and fry onions until golden. Season the flour and use half to coat the pork. Fry these lightly until brown on each side and then remove.

Chop the mushrooms and fry lightly, mixing in with the onion. Turn down to a very low heat, stir in the remaining seasoned flour to make a basic roux with the butter and then gradually add the cider, stirring all the while. Bring to the boil for a minute. Season with a little salt and pepper, return the pork to the pan, cover and simmer on a low heat for 20 minutes or until the pork is tender.

Now stir in the cream and chopped chives. Serve with boiled new potatoes and runner or French beans. Bon appetit!

Chicken or Rabbit with Cider

As a variant on the above pork recipe, try using chicken breasts or legs or similar joints from rabbit. The onion can be replaced with several fat cloves of garlic which should be very lightly fried and then removed, to be added and mashed in once the cider sauce has been made.

Fish in Cider

Serves 4: preparation and cooking time 40 mins or less.

Ingredients
¼ litre or ½ pint dry cider
4 white fish steaks or fillets
30g or 1oz butter
Salt and pepper
Juice of half a lemon
1 beef tomato
60g or 2oz mushrooms
30g or 1oz plain flour
Tablespoon chopped parsley

Method
Put the fish in a greased baking dish and top with sliced tomatoes and mushrooms. Season with salt and pepper, add lemon juice and pour in the cider. Cover the dish with a lid or foil and bake in a moderately hot oven for about 20–25 minutes/microwave 8 minutes.

Drain the liquid off from the fish, keeping this hot. Melt the butter gently in a heavy saucepan, stir in the flour to make a basic roux and now add in the reserved cider/fish liquid to make the sauce, stirring all the while and bringing to the boil for 1 minute.

Pour the sauce over the fish and garnish with the chopped parsley. Serve with mashed or boiled potatoes and preferred vegetables.

Hereford Cider Sauce with Boiled Bacon or Ham

This is another delicious cider recipe, very quickly made.

Ingredients
½ litre or 1 pint cider
1 boiling bacon or ham
2–3 tablespoons pork or lamb dripping
30g or 1oz plain flour
300ml or ¾ pint vegetable or meat stock
2 cloves
1 bay leaf
Salt and pepper

Method
Cook the boiling bacon or ham. Melt the pork or lamb dripping in a heavy saucepan, stir in the flour to a smooth dark roux. Add the vegetable or meat stock, stirring all the while, and bring to the boil to thicken the sauce. Now add the cider, cloves, bay leaf and season. Mix thoroughly. Pour the sauce over the bacon or ham and serve with preferred vegetables.

There is a quite unique pleasure in turning the thread to exert pressure on apple pulp, whence the juice comes gushing out. It is very good to taste and drink in its own right.

14 Preserving Pure Apple Juice

The apple juice we press doesn't have to be fermented to cider – it can simply be drunk and is so much more delicious than any commercial product you could ever buy. It really is a case of tasting is believing. Even if you have little interest in cider, but have apples and like apple juice, then owning or making a press is a must.

Once again, this pressing of the apple juice could take place at a small scale or 'multi-family' or community level, where the labour and the pleasure and the juice are shared out among the participants. The best type of juice for drinking is sweet and yet has a nice acid dimension, as well as all the other subtle flavours. Anywhere between 60–70% sweet dessert apples with the balance of the 'cooker' type will produce an excellent juice. However, make certain that all fruit is sound, that all apples that are mouldy or have been in contact with mouldy apples are discarded without compromise. Cut out the worst of internal rot and bruising (see Appendix 6).

Freshly pressed apple juice can be drunk for up to 4–5 days after pressing, providing the juice is kept in a refrigerator. Any quantities that are not going to be drunk within this period have to be preserved *within a few hours of pressing* if the full flavour is to be kept and you want to drink it over the months after making. It is *not* a question of simply putting it in a cupboard somewhere and taking what you want, when you want; it will have begun to ferment long before you have drunk a fraction of it, and in a closed vessel would run the risk of explosion!

There are two basic methods of preserving the apple juice. Both are excellent. What is more, neither involve the use of preservatives or any additives so you know that the juice is pure.

Freezing

By far the most convenient vessels to use for freezing are either empty commercial apple or other fruit juice boxes, with the 'cut spout' sealed with extra-sticky tape or by other means. You can also use small juice or squash drink plastic bottles of about 1 litre capacity (or larger if you drink a lot of juice).

Do not, under any circumstances, freeze the juice in glass bottles. Whichever other vessel you choose to freeze the juice in, you must remember to leave a 5cm (2in.) space at the top of the juice to allow for expansion upon freezing.

The advantage of this method is that it is quick, convenient and produces juice upon thawing even months later that is as delicious as when it came out of the press. The disadvantage of the method is that it can use up a lot of freezer space and you have to remember to take it out beforehand to allow time for thawing. Once thawed, consume within 4–5 days at most, providing it is kept in a refrigerator.

Pasteurisation

Pasteurisation is a technique which kills the micro-organisms (including the wild yeasts, and breaks down their enzymes) in the apple juice that bring about fermentations. Once, pasteurised, the juice can be kept in bottles indefinitely and is immediately available for drinking, unlike frozen juice. The process does, however, involve a little investment of time and care to do it properly, and does alter the flavour of the juice very slightly.

Clean glass bottles are needed, either the old quart bottles with ceramic tops (or later plastic alternatives) and rubber seal, or modern fizzy soft drink bottles with internal plastic-coated metal tops. Other similar type of bottle such as the 'clip top' beer bottles can also be used. Make sure that all seals and tops are in good condition and sterilised with boiling water, otherwise the juice will spoil.

The bottles are filled to within 1–2cm of the top with juice and then placed in a hot water bath which has been heated and held at 70°C (the precise pasteurising temperature is actually 72.4°C). The water in the bath must immerse as much of the bottles as possible so that all of the juice is subjected to a temperature of 70°C. Do not put too many bottles into the bath at any one time since you need to establish a good water/heat circulation. The juice in the bottles must be held at this temperature – a standard thermometer will be needed – for 30 minutes. Confirm that the juice in the bottles has indeed been subjected to this temperature for this period of time by carefully lowering the (cleaned) thermometer into the juice in one of the bottles two-thirds of the way down.

If you have judged the correct level to fill the bottles up to, even allowing for expansion, there will be no running over. If a little does, however, do not worry. At the end of the 30 minutes remove the bottles carefully, screw on or down the caps, place the bottles on their side without touching each other and as they cool down a sterile vacuum seal will be created inside each bottle. Wipe the outside of the bottles free of any stickiness and store in a cool, dark place. Use when wanted.

Once opened, the juice will keep well for 4–5 days in a refrigerator. A thermostatically controlled pasteuriser can be bought which makes the job much easier and certainly the relatively modest outlay would be justified if you have large quantities of juice. Alternatively, both the cost and usage of the device could be shared out among a number of people – another opportunity for communal enterprise (and a little party!).

15 Making Cider Vinegar

Cider vinegar, as any chef will vouchsafe, is a valued culinary commodity. Some regard it as possibly superior to wine vinegar in the making of vinaigrette, and it is excellent in marinades. It is also reputed to have wide ranging health benefits when taken in various recipes and/or as part of a daily diet.

Making cider vinegar from dry cider

Vinegar is a dilute solution of ethanoic (acetic) acid – on average about 5% – which comes about by the oxidation of the alcohol in the fermented product.

Making cider vinegar is a simple if somewhat lengthy process at a domestic level, since it uses the relatively inefficient (but practical at this level) Orléans process. The cider you start off with needs to be relatively strong in the first place, say 8–9%, since using this process will only give you a vinegar at about 5% acid level. It is important for pickling purposes to have the vinegar at this degree of ethanoic (acetic) acid since below this value there is a risk of microbial spoilage of the preserved food. On the other hand, cider vinegar is not usually used for pickling, and if you are intending using the vinegar for marinades, vinaigrette, or for drinking or as part of a diet, it is perfectly possible to start off with a much weaker cider and turn it into a cider vinegar having an acid level below the accepted level of 5%.

There are basically two approaches. Ferment the natural juice out completely to dry cider, having racked off from the bulk of the settled lees when the fermentation begins to slow down. Add sugar as recommended at the first racked stage, unless you started off with a particularly sweet juice. Rack again when the cider is once again dry, clear or slightly hazy and then pour into a vessel – barrel, plastic fermenter, demi-john – up to two-thirds, leaving a good head of air above the cider. Lay the barrel on its side if possible to maximise the surface area of cider to air in order to promote the oxidation. If you can't lay it on its side, don't worry. Note that the cider *should not be sulphited*, nor should it have been sulphited in any way prior to this point since this would inhibit the acetifying bacteria. Now put across the mouth of the vessel a loose mesh cloth, scrim or muslin (do not plug) to allow air free access. *Leave in a distinctly warm place* over the coming weeks and months.

This process may be speeded up by buying from an obliging small producer of vinegar a culture known as a 'vinegar mother', basically a gelatinous material of *acetobacter* responsible for the acetification process. It used to be common in buying what was then unpasteurised malt, wine or cider vinegar to see the mother floating about in the bottom of the bottle. The bacteria are also found in any hazy vinegar you may come across. In either case introduce the culture (the mother or

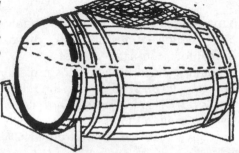

Making cider vinegar in a barrel by the Orléans process. Notice the level of the cider and the loose cloth over the open bung hole to allow free air passage.

the hazy vinegar) to the body of the cider and leave once again in as warm place.

If you cannot get hold of a vinegar mother, or any hazy vinegar, then you can try first culturing your own acetifying bacteria by exposing an open jar of dry unsulphited cider to the air for several weeks. Smell and taste this at intervals to identify the unmistakeable vinegary quality which forms as a consequence of the wild bacteria in the air and then use this to culture the main body of cider as described above.

The idea from now on is to expose the cider to as much air as possible for two or three months, or longer if necessary. The alcohol will be oxidised by the *acetobacter* which proliferates in the presence of air and forms the ethanoic (acetic) acid to produce the cider vinegar. Smell and taste the developing product from time to time to gauge how the vinegar is forming. When it tastes nicely vinegary and doesn't seem to be getting any more so, bottle either into corked wine bottles or screw-top bottles and store. (As an added precaution against any possibility of later fermentation in bottle due to residual sugars and yeasts in the vinegar, you may wish to pasteurise: adopt the same procedures for juice preservation or cider pasteurisation.)

Remember, never use the same vessels and equipment for making vinegar as you use for making cider. Keep cidermaking and vinegar making separate and try not to perform them even physically close together, since you are concerned to prevent any possibility of acetification of your cider.

Making cider vinegar by the Orléans process using a glass demi-john

More of that fine weather!

Appendix 1: Glossary of Terms

ABV (Alcohol by Volume) Measure of the alcoholic content of a beverage, usually expressed as the percentage (%) of alcohol by volume.

Acetification Process whereby some or all of the formed alcohol is oxidised to ethanoic (acetic) acid which gives the cider a sharp vinegary taste.

Acidity Measure of the sharpness in the juice or cider, measured quantitatively by pH. This is a crucial characteristic to acquire at the correct level for a good cider.

Aerobic fermentation Fermentation by yeasts or other organisms requiring air.

Alcohol: ethanol (ethyl alcohol) This is the main product formed from sugars by yeast during fermentation.

Ammonium phosphate   Nutrient for yeast supplying vital nitrogen (N) and phosphorus (P)

Anaerobic Fermentation   Fermentation by yeasts or other organisms which occurs in the absence of air.

Aspartame   Commonly used artificial sweetener in the food industry. Sometimes used by cidermakers because it is non-fermentable.

Autolysis   Breaking open of dead yeast cells (which then become prone to bacterial decay and potential spoilage of cider if left on these yeast lees).

Bentonite   Diatomaceous clay used as a very effective fining.

Bittersharp   Class of cider apple reflecting the balance of tannin to acid.

Bittersweet   Class of cider apple reflecting the balance of tannin to sugar.

Campden tablets   Convenient form of sulphiting with potassium metabisulphite to give the equivalent of 50ppm (parts per million) of sulphur dioxide to a gallon of juice or cider. Used for sterilisation or stabilisation of cider.

Carbon dioxide   The other principal fermentation product; colourless, odourless, non-toxic gas which also provides condition for cider.

'Cheese'   Built-up pack comprising layers of apple pulp, wrapped in cloths, each layer separated by wooden or plastic racks. The whole is then pressed to release the juice.

Citric acid   Principal acid of citrus fruit; sometimes used in cidermaking to adjust acid levels. Also used in conjunction with sodium/potassium metabisulphite to release free sulphur dioxide for effective sterilisation.

Condition   Term used to describe drinks that have acquired by a secondary fermentation small amounts of dissolved carbon dioxide i.e. a pleasant sparkle which also brings out the aromas of a drink.

Cuvage A form of steeping or maceration in which apple pulp is left in open-topped barrels in the cold for a day to promote juice formation and induce enzymic changes prior to process of pressing and keeving.

Demi-john Common name for a 1-gallon glass fermentation jar.

Dry In the context of cider the term describes a drink formed by the complete or near-complete fermentation of all sugars i.e. with a specific gravity (SG) of between 1000 and 1005. Completely unsweet.

Enzymes Naturally occurring (or synthetically prepared) protein catalysts which are responsible for almost all changes in brewing (and every other living process!). These are the critical biological substances, for example, that yeasts use to convert sugars to alcohol.

Fermentation Conversion of sugars to alcohol, carbon dioxide and water by yeasts or other micro-organisms.

Filtration Clarifying hazy or cloudy ciders using filters comprising of powders, papers or pads.

Fining Removal (by depositing out) of fine suspended solids which are responsible for hazes and cloudiness in some ciders. This process is brought about by the addition of finings drawn from a whole range of different sources (often animal or vegetable in origin).

Gelatine An effective and commonly used fining.

Hydrometer An instrument used for measuring the specific gravity (SG) of a juice, or a developing or completely fermented out drink. The instrument gives a measure of the dissolved sugar in the liquid. Usually two types: brewer's and winemaker's, this latter being used in cidermaking.

Keeving Technique used in traditional cidermaking whereby enzymic changes in apple juice are promoted to arrive at a clear, low-nutrient juice which can be very slowly fermented to naturally sweet ciders. The technique is often associated with French cidermaking where the addition of sugar or other sweeteners is proscribed.

Lactose   The principal sugar found in milk. Can be obtained from brewing supplies for use as a means of artificially sweetening ciders. Has the advantage of being unfermentable by *Saccharomyces* yeasts.

Lees   The solid deposits of fruit and/or yeast settling to the bottom of a vessel during and after fermentation.

Malic acid   The principal acid found in apples.

Malolactic fermentation   Slow *lactobacillus* (not yeasts) induced fermentation of ciders (and wines) which, in warmer conditions, can convert the harsher malic acid in a cider to the softer lactic acid thereby producing a maturer, more palatable drink.

Manucube   Simple 'bag-in-a-box' means of dispensing wine or cider which prevents the ingress of air to acetify the drink. Cider stored in a manucube can be drawn off when it is wanted over several weeks without the risk of spoilage.

Metabisulphite   Commonly used term for sodium or potassium metabisulphite used as the most common forms of sterilising vessels and stabilising ciders. The substances release sulphur dioxide in the vessel of drink, which kills unwanted micro-organisms.

'Mock'   Another term for a 'cheese' (see 'Cheese') but one where the apple pulp is 'bound up' with straw instead of wrapped in polyester cloths and separated by racks. Obsolete or near-obsolete practice now.

Naturally conditioned   An alcoholic beverage which has acquired carbonation or a sparkle by a natural secondary fermentation occurring in the storage vessel.

Oxidation   Particular type of chemical or biochemical reaction, often requiring the presence of oxygen in air, facilitated by enzymes of micro-organisms or other chemical agents. For example, the rapid coloration of apple juice once formed is due to the onset of oxidation of tannin in the juice. The acetification of the alcohol (ethanol) to vinegar (ethanoic acid) is another oxidation, sometimes chemical, sometimes biochemical in origin.

Pasteurisation   A technique of holding liquids at 72.4°C for a while in order to preserve them discovered by Louis Pasteur (1822–1895). At this temperature the flavour of a beverage (e.g. apple juice or cider) is not demonstrably affected, but most of the micro-organisms responsible for spoilage are killed. Providing a sterile vacuum seal is created above the drink, it will keep indefinitely.

Patulin   Name given to a complex of toxins created by mouldy or decaying apples (and other fruit). Such fruit should never be used in making apple juice. Now believed to be destroyed during fermentation processes.

Pectin   Natural carbohydrate found in apples (and many other fruits) responsible for helping jam set and, annoyingly, the formation of a number of hazes in cider.

Pectolytic enzyme   Usually available as the synthetically prepared or extracted enzyme of that naturally occurring in apples. Pectin hazes (see above) are not that common, but in certain fruit and circumstances will be formed. Addition of synthetic pectolytic enzyme at the outset of fermentation can often forestall the chance of hazes.

Press cloth   Squares of terylene, nylon, or other polyester used to wrap up the apple pulp (e.g. when making the 'cheese' or 'pack') prior to pressing.

Racking   Siphoning of the cider from the lees when the fermentation has finished or all but finished in order to clear and stabilise the final product during storage.

Remuage   From the French meaning to move or twist. Used in making so-called 'champagne cider'. This is the technique used to work the yeast down onto the cork of the inverted bottle, prior to freezing and removal of this sediment plug.

'Riddling'   Same as 'remuage'.

Scratter   Type of mill (hand or power-operated) with interlocking teeth that converts the apples into a fine grained milled state prior to pressing.

Sorbitol   Artificial non-fermentable sweetener.

Specific Gravity (SG)   Gives a quantitative measure of the amount of sugar present in a juice or beverage. Other dissolved materials all contribute to the overall measured SG value but sugar is by far and away the principal contributor. Knowing the SG values of starting juice and fermented product enables the cidermaker to calculate how much alcohol is present or how much more sugar to add for a desired strength.

Still   In the context of cider the term refers to a lack of any form of carbonation in the drink i.e. it has no sparkle.

Sulphiting   General term used whenever a juice or cider is subject to treatment by a source of sulphur dioxide i.e. the addition of sodium/potassium metabisulphite, or Campden tablets, or free sulphur dioxide for purposes of sterilisation or stabilisation.

Taint   Spoilage of cider by picking up trace flavours usually from unclean, inappropriate or outlawed vessels.

Tannin   A substance present in apples (and other fruit and many plants) which confers an important astringency to the cider. Crab apples and cider apples have good levels of tannin and it is crucial to get the correct balance of tannin for a good cider.

Ullage   This is the difference between the volume capacity of the vessel e.g. a cask and the actual volume of cider (or beer/wine) in the cask. In other words, it is the space above the level of the cider in a storage vessel.

Vinegar   Approximately 5% solution of ethanoic (acetic) acid formed by the bacterial oxidation of the alcohol in the cider or wine.

Yeast   Generally taken as the micro-organism *Saccharomyces* ('sugar fungus') responsible for fermentation i.e. the conversion of sugar to alcohol, water and carbon dioxide in the making of alcoholic beverages. There are many yeasts, some of them spoilage organisms.

Appendix 2: Making Perry

Perry from pears is less well known than cider, but is a most distinctive drink and much prized among its many followers. Especially for the small producer and retailer, cider and perry usually go hand in hand. Making perry follows exactly the same principles as those for cidermaking, although it is difficult to make good perry without using genuine perry pear varieties. There are many fine examples of these with wonderful names such as Malvern Hills, Green Horse, Tumper, Merrylegs and Dumbleton Huffcap. Butt is another very commonly used perry pear variety. Such fruit is unrecognisable as a dessert pear, but contains a balance of flavours and, not least, high proportions of tannins which makes for a fine end product. Unlike apples, perry pears (indeed all pears) ripen much earlier, and few have any keeping properties. It is important once they are harvested to press them immediately and to get the fermentation underway.

If you would like to try making perry but have only a selection of fruit that is of a dessert type rather than actually perry pears, then don't despair of making the drink but recognise at the outset the inadequacies of the juice such fruit will produce and adjust this before fermentation. The fruit will be very juicy, sweet and contain the usual selection of esters, but upon tasting it will be quite remarkably bland and insipid, and if fermented would produce a completely undistinguished product. Therefore, adjust for acid and tannin by the addition of these (as indicated in Chapter 9) and you are much more likely to end up with a product to your liking.

If you feel that the sweetness is lacking also, then add white sugar as a syrup as indicated for adjusting apple juice in Chapter 10 (or use the cold racking technique if you are opposed to the addition of sweeteners) either prior to fermentation, or after the first racking stage. In our experience also, perry made from dessert pears experiences more difficulty in clearing than cider, and because of this it is advisable to add pectolytic enzyme at the rate of 1 tablespoon per gallon of juice to facilitate clarification. To some extent this clearing problem is a reflection of over-ripe fruit, but you will be extremely fortunate if you can prepare your juice from fruit which has been caught just at the right point.

Naturally, if you have access to genuine perry pear varieties you should be able to make excellent examples of the drink, but in general the best perries are of the single varietal types because pears do not blend well, unlike apples.

Perries are more conventionally produced sweet or medium sweet (rarely ever dry) because many varieties contain significant natural levels of non-fermentable sorbitol. They are also quite often naturally conditioned in bottle (or artificially carbonated). Follow the procedures for producing these types of drink as indicated for those corresponding ciders in Chapter 10.

And what of pear and apple trees? The pear tree has a lovely upward curving crown whose display of blossom is a very distinctive feature of the Herefordshire and Worcestershire landscapes in Britain – a blossom which is out in all its finery weeks before that of the apple. While the perry pear tree can take many years to come into fruit, you can still find examples bearing in abundance two or even three hundred years later, when the apple tree has long been dead.

Appendix 3: The Malolactic Fermentation

This minor fermentation is usually a welcome prospect to any cidermaker or winemaker. It can either occur in the bulk racked-off cider if left for any period of time, or in the bottle in the case of still ciders. It is usually welcome because the fermentation alters the sharp acidity of the predominant malic acid from the apples to the less acidic lactic acid, creating a rounder, smoother character to the cider. A cider already low in acidity can, if this fermentation goes on too long, turn insipid, but this is an unusual outcome.

The fermentation is brought about not by yeasts, but by species of *lactobacillus* bacteria (of the types cultured in yoghurt making) and apart from its 'smoothing' effect it can also leave an otherwise still cider slightly 'spritzy' with the carbon dioxide given off, so that there is a general enlivening and freshening effect upon the drink.

Very often the malolactic fermentation takes place quietly and inconspicuously in the spring when the weather warms up a little and the bacterial population has grown sufficiently for the change to take place. It is rare for there to be any visible sign of bacterial deposit because of the size of the micro-organism. The drink remains clear throughout. Having said all this, the malolactic fermentation is by no means guaranteed to actually occur, and usually it is a question of good fortune if it takes place at all. It will almost certainly not occur if the young cider has been sulphited as a matter of course in suppressing spoilage agents prior to storage. Nowadays, it is possible to purchase malolactic bacteria cultures and, if you wish to try and bring about this fermentation deliberately, then you will need to add the culture along with nutrients to the young racked off cider and bring this into a warmer environment for a period of time.

Appendix 4: Using the Hydrometer

A hydrometer will measure the specific gravity (SG) of a liquid; it is used in making beer, wine and cider where it offers an approximate measure of the dissolved sugars and the potential alcohol obtainable from those sugars.

The specific gravity of the natural juice (or wort/must in the case of beer/wine) is sometimes referred to as the original gravity (OG). The instrument can do no better than offer us approximate measures of the sugar and potential alcohol because all the other dissolved materials – the acids, the developing alcohol, the suspended proteins of the yeast and apples etc. and not just the sugar – make their individual contributions to the measured specific gravity. However, the hydrometer works because the dissolved sugar is by far and away the principal contributor to the measured SG.

Most cidermaking never involves, or needs to involve, a hydrometer. The eye, watching out for all the indicators marking the progress of fermentation, and the practice of tasting the cider at appropriate stages are, in the long run, probably better judges than a hydrometer.

However, the instrument has its uses and some people like to have a quantitative measure of the fermentation progress and the formed alcohol.

A hydrometer can:

- Indicate the approximate level of sugars in the original pressed juice, and therefore by reading the scale, the potential alcohol obtainable from these natural sugars alone assuming complete fermentation.
- Indicate the quantity of (white) sugar to be added in order to achieve a particular alcoholic strength.
- Show the SG of the final fermented-out cider and therefore the approximate residual sugar (tiny remaining unfermented quantities) in the cider.
- Show the approximate alcoholic strength of the final cider by deducting the final sugar level from the total sugars (comprised of the original plus the added) and reading off the % alcohol scale.

An example

If our OG happened to be 1060 = 708g (1lb 9oz) sugar per gallon
Added sugar at racked off stage = 170g (6oz) sugar per gallon
Total possible fermentable sugar = 878g (1lb 15oz) sugar per gallon
Suppose final SG to be 1005 = 28g (1oz) sugar per gallon
Total sugar actually fermented = 850g (1lb 14oz) sugar per gallon
Final alcoholic strength of cider = 9.5%

Our final cider is likely to have a %-alcohol (ABV) less than this since we didn't take into account the slight volume changes upon racking, but nevertheless this is quite a strong cider. This is not so surprising since the juice we started off with in this example at SG 1060 must have been very sweet.

Taking readings off a hydrometer are notoriously difficult and if intending using the instrument, it is better simply to accept approximate readings than to struggle for greater accuracy and end up both defeated and exhausted! You will need a tall, narrow-diameter, clear-walled specimen vessel of a height greater than the length of the hydrometer. Glass measuring cylinders are the best pieces of apparatus, though improvising one of these from a clear plastic fruit squash bottle is possible. Readings should be taken from the bottom of the meniscus – if you can even see the menicus, for therein lies the basic problem of taking readings. Don't worry! Cidermaking like most of the best things in life is actually a craft that is best exercised through use of all the senses, along with developing judgements and experience.

Syphon off the juice or cider whose SG you wish to measure into the thoroughly clean and dry specimen vessel, more or less up to the top. Lower the hydrometer carefully into the liquid, restrain it from rotating and touching the sides of the vessel, wait for it to remain perfectly still and then read off the SG. Return the juice/cider to the fermentation vessel. Rinse and dry both specimen vessel and hydrometer.

Approximate SG values to prospective alcoholic strengths are given on page 57.

Appendix 5: Pasteurisation and Stabilisation of Cider

Pasteurisation has already been dealt with in the context of preserving apple juice for drinking. However, it is also often used as a stabilising treatment for cider (and perry) – the practice being, once again, a vexed question amongst cidermakers.

Purists will have none of it, placing it in the same category as sulphiting, and the question of additives, including the use of cultured yeasts and the role of white sugar and other artificial sweeteners. Indeed, among many cidermakers, the definition of real cider revolves around these issues. The anguishing to some extent is perfectly understandable given that most commercial ciders can be subject to some pretty grisly practices.

For others, who would consider themselves to be perfectly genuine small-scale 'traditional' cidermakers, pasteurisation represents a reliable and safe means of rendering their ciders completely stable, and is usually used in conjunction with artificial conditioning (carbonation) of their ciders, especially medium sweet/sweet ciders. For such makers, especially if they are retailing the product, there are clear advantages to this approach. Naturally conditioned medium sweet/ sweet ciders which are 'live' in deliberately having tiny amounts of yeast in the bottle do run a small risk of burst bottles, a possibility which will increase the longer the bottle remains unopened. If the bottle remains on a shelf, unsold, let us say, for some considerable period of time, there is a palpable risk here. Indeed, any 'traditional' hazy cider, perhaps retaining trace quantities of yeast, is potentially unstable and runs a risk which can be removed by pasteurisation. Good quality pasteurisers of various capacities are available from reputable commercial suppliers.

Of course, some cider producers, large and small, obviate the need for pasteurisation when making a medium sweet/sweet cider by sweetening a dry cider with saccharine, aspartame, sorbitol or lactose, all of which are unfermentable: a practice which is an abomination to purists. Against such considerations is the fact that there can be no question that pasteurisation does alter (and to our minds, impair) the flavour of the cider. For the small-scale maker of cider for domestic or social use, there is probably simply no need ever to get involved with the process. The small-scale retailer will have to decide on the merits and demerits.

The traditional means of stabilising cider, and still used by many cidermakers, is simply to store in bulk long enough and in a cold enough environment, before finally racking off from any residual lees. This applies equally to dry cider as to any other cider retaining a residual sweetness. The possibility of re-fermentation, however, is always there in the back of the mind which is why many cidermakers prefer to pasteurise.

Alternatively, either sulphur dioxide as metabisulphite or Campden tablets equivalent to 100ppm (2 Campden tablets per gallon) can be used to kill any yeast present. A further alternative is to add 1 Campden tablet with 1g of potassium sorbate per gallon, a mixture which is sometimes sold as a proprietary 'stopping' compound. There are others also retailed.

Appendix 6: A Note on Patulin

Patulin is a natural toxin produced by various moulds that infect apples. It is also found in other mouldy fruit. Ministry of Agriculture, Fisheries & Food (MAFF) guidelines as to the recommended level in pressed apple juice is 50ug patulin/kg juice or cider (50 parts per billion). The most recent research seems to point to the toxin being destroyed during fermentation, so that cider itself may very well be free of patulin. It is probably better, however, to observe the precautions outlined below anyway, though it is certainly essential in the case of any unfermented juice or juice products made for personal consumption or those being retailed.

Although most of the patulin is found in the mouldy part of an apple, even the sound-looking adjacent parts may be infected with the toxin. For this reason it is recommended that any apple being used to make juice or cider that shows evidence of mould should be discarded without compromise. Any adjacent apples that have spent any time in contact with mouldy fruit should also, as a precaution, be discarded even though they may appear to be sound. Bruised apples, on the other hand, are not necessarily infected at all, though being damaged, the flesh immediately becomes more open to mould attack. If you have a superabundance of apples and wish to be cautious, then discard bruised fruit; otherwise, use your judgement. If the fruit is deeply bruised, discard it; if recently and lightly bruised, you will probably wish to use it. The above levels of patulin are only guidelines and at the moment there is no cheap test available to determine the levels of patulin in juice although MAFF is currently developing one. If you intend retailing any of your juice or cider, you should be aware of the need to comply with the *Food Safety Act 1990*. For the small-scale producer, providing you can demonstrate that you have taken reasonable precautions in limiting the level of patulin in the juice (a process of 'due diligence') this may serve as acceptable – though not necessarily successful – defence if for any reason should you ever be subject to prosecution.

The point about patulin is that it has always been with us inasmuch as we have always had mouldy apples! There is no need to become alarmist about it. For many of us, we probably take in higher concentrations of pollutants every time we take a breath in some city environments, or when we take a glass of water from our domestic water supply. Yes, the particular toxin in mouldy fruit has been identified, given a name and some of its effects investigated enough for us to be aware that we should minimise its levels in such things as natural apple products. The truth, however, is that we will probably never be able to remove patulin entirely from apple juice and ciders.

Observe the following code:

- Discard apples that are in any way mouldy or have been in contact with mouldy apples.
- Wash apples thoroughly before extracting juice from them.

Apples here are infected with a variety of moulds and should not be used for either juice or cidermaking.

Appendix 7: Cleaning and Sterilising Wooden Casks/Barrels

Cleaning and sterilising these wooden vessels requires special consideration to make certain they are fit for fermentation and storage of cider. A number of options are available depending on the type of cask under consideration.

Preparation of new casks

Wash out with several gallons of warm water. Make up brine by dissolving 8oz salt in 2 pints of hot water for a 5-gallon barrel, increasing the quantity for higher volumes. Add to the barrel, fill up with hot water (do not use boiling water as this can open up staves). Leave for a week, open up, rinse out well with cold water until free of salt.

Cleaning and sterilising soiled casks

(1) Remove any gross dirt/deposit on the inside of barrels by adding several handfuls of small stone chippings or using a length of brass chain and shake thoroughly, repeatedly with hot water. Remove chain. In the case of stone chippings, remove by repeated swilling out with hot water.

(2) Make up a solution of sodium carbonate (washing soda) at the rate of 4oz/125g to a gallon of cold water. For larger barrels (e.g. 36/42 gallon oak barrels) you will probably need to make up about 20 gallons of this solution.

(3) Pour the soda solution into the barrel, bung tightly, slosh around at regular intervals over the next two days.

(4) Empty, rinse out thoroughly with copious quantities of cold water.

(5) Prepare a solution of citric acid at the rate of 1oz/30g to a gallon of cold water. Add this in sufficient volume to the barrels to neutralise any residual sodium carbonate. Swirl around thoroughly.

(6) Drain and rinse thoroughly with copious quantities of water.

(7) Drain, dry, bung up for a week.

(8) Make up a sterilising solution: 3g sodium or potassium metabisulphite (or 6 Campden tablets) with 10g citric acid dissolved in 1 pint of water. Be careful – this solution releases a lot of sulphur dioxide which should not be inhaled!

(9) Add this solution to the barrel, bung, swirl solution round. Keep barrel bunged until required for use.

(10) Rinse out barrel with copious quantities of cold water, after which your vessel will be sweet and sterile and ready for use.

As an alternative to the use of sodium carbonate as the cleaning agent, sodium hypochlorite as the active ingredient in domestic bleach can also be used. Make up a solution by dissolving 1fl oz/25g of domestic bleach in 1 gallon of cold water. Use this in the above sequence instead of the sodium carbonate, but otherwise follow the procedure.

Steam treatment of barrels

A further way of treating particularly soiled barrels is to steam treat them. First, rinse out the barrel with boiling water but keep this moving in order to prevent opening of the staves. The barrel can now be steamed by connecting a plastic or rubber pipe to a pressure cooker. Remove the pressure relief valve, connect the pipe, and steam for about 30 minutes by putting the pipe through the bung hole. After this, rinse well with hot water, and then either treat with salt as above, or with a sterilising solution, finally rinsing out with copious quantities of cold water.

This may seem like a rather complicated process, but while wood is an excellent material to have for cider vessels, it is prone to getting dirty and infected; old barrels will particularly need the above treatment. Don't forget to use your nose to finally gauge the 'sweetness' of your barrels after the above cleaning and sterilisation. If something is still not quite right and there is still a little mustiness or sourness there, you will need to repeat the above procedure.

Don't immediately sniff at vessels to check for sweetness after the use of sulphiting agents – use your nose only at the end of the final rinsing out session.

Barrels that are not being used for any length of time should be stored with a pint or so of metabisulphite/citric acid solution (stage 8 above), rinsing this out thoroughly with cold water when the barrel is about to be used again. This will always ensure that the inside of the barrel remains sterile and 'sweet'.

Barrels that have recently contained rum or brandy or sherry are to be prized, since cider stored in these acquires special 'vintage' characteristics. Such barrels should not be cleaned out for obvious reasons.

To increase the lifetime of barrels and to prevent their drying out with consequent loss of cider, the *exterior* can be treated with linseed oil, say, every three years or so.

Appendix 8: Useful Information and Addresses

Cidermaking equipment and accessories
Vigo Ltd, Dunkeswell Airfield, Dunkeswell, Honiton,
Devon EX14 4LF
(Fruit Juice & Cider Production equipment, services and much more)
www.vigoltd.com
Cidermaking Associations
Three Counties Cider & Perry Association, Gregg's Pit, Much
Marcle, Ledbury, Herefordshire HR8 2NL
National Association of Cider Makers
info@cideruk.com
The South West of England Cidermakers Association, Green Valley
Cider, Marsh Barton Farm, Clyst St. George, Exeter,
Devon EX3 0QH
Other important organisations
Common Ground, Gold Hill House, 21 High Street, Shaftesbury,
Dorset SP7 8JE
info@commonground.org.uk
Apple/CAMRA, Camra Ltd, 230 Hatfield Road, St. Albans,
Herts AL1 4LW
Soil Association, Bristol House, 40-56 Victoria Street,
Bristol BS1 6BY
www.soilassociation.org

Museums

The Cider Museum & King Offa Distillery, Pomona Place,
Hereford HR4 OLW

Cidermaking courses

The Green Wood Trust, Station Road, Coalbrookdale, Telford,
Shropshire TF8 7DR

Pershore & Hindlip College, Peter Mitchell, Hindlip,
Worcester WR3 8SS

Rufford Craft Centre, Rufford Country Park, Ollerton, Newark,
Nottinghamshire NG22 9DF
www.ruffordceramiccentre.org.uk

Cidermaking demonstrations

Big Apple Association, Woodcroft, Putley, Ledbury, Herefordshire
HR8 2RD

Apple Trees & Other Fruit Tree Nurseries

Thornhayes Nursery, St Andrews Wood, Dulford, Cullompton, Devon
EX152DF
www.thornhayes-nursery.co.uk

Dolau-Hirion Fruit Tree Nursery, Paul Davis, Capel Isaac, Landeilo,
Carmarthenshire SA19 7TG

H P Bulmer, The Cider Mills, Plough Lane, Hereford HR4 OLE

Useful reading

Making, Using & Enjoying Sweet & Hard Cider by Annie Proulx
& Lou Nichols (Stag Communications, Vermont).

Cidermaking by Michael B Quinion (Shire Publications Ltd, 1982).

The Good Cider Guide CAMRA publication (published annually)

Fermented Beverage Production by Andrew Lea & John Pigott
(Blackie, Chapman & Hall, 1995).

Conversion Table – Weights, measures, temperature

Conversion		
From	To	Multiply by
fl. oz.	ml. or cc.	28
ml. or cc.	fl. oz.	0.0357
litres (l)	gallons	0.22
gallons	litres	4.546
ounces (oz)	grammes (g)	33.333
grammes (g)	ounces (oz)	0.03
kilogrammes (kg)	pounds (lb)	2.205
pounds (lb)	kilogrammes (kg)	0.4536
Fahrenheit (°F)	Celsius/Centigrade (°C)	subtract 32, multiply by 5, divide by 9
Celsius/Centigrade (°C)	Fahrenheit (°F)	multiply by 9, divide by 5, add 32

Index